A
Vanished
Road

Books by Veena Schlegel

Glimpses of my Master
A Mountain in China

https://3booksblog.wordpress.com/

https://www.facebook.com/pg/booksbyveena/posts

A Vanished Road

by
Veena Schlegel

To Andy and Francine

Hope you enjoy these
travels!

love Veena

Acknowledgements

Many thanks to dear friends
Bhagawati Moriss for proofing help,
Punya Kaufeler for creating my website,
and Trish Sharpe for sharing her photographs,
more of which can be seen on my website

Contents

A Vanished Road
introduction

Introduction

A Vanished Road is a travel story. It is an account of a journey overland through mid-eastern countries to India in 1971. The world then was a very different place to what it is today.

The countries I and five travelling companions travelled through – by train, boat, bus, local indescribable vehicles and sometimes on foot – were untouched and unspoilt by tourism and other international influences. Television was still a novelty in western countries; here it was unknown. For most of the local people, the hippies travelling through, breaking that later quite well-trodden trail, were the first westerners they had ever seen.

There were no maps or guidebooks. The only guide was the hippie grapevine and the pointing of a local's finger. Toby and Marianne Wheeler, founders of the famous Lonely Planet guidebooks, traversed this road a year later – a journey which provided the inspiration for the beginning of their venture. English was rare, other languages unknown, so communication took place on a different level – via the heart, via intuition. It was always a guessing game.

Our experiences were varied and unique. Sometimes we were met by innocent interest and open-hearted generosity, sometimes by infuriatingly deliberate stonewalling, sometimes by suspicion and hostility. We needed to keep our wits about us and be very patient. It was usually a friendly smile and a calm centeredness that got us through.

The journey was physically and emotionally demanding but the reward was a deeply touching and life-changing experience which cannot now be repeated. With the events of the last few decades – tragic in the case of Afghanistan – this road, with its unique flavour, has vanished forever.

London to Istanbul – by train

travelling companions found, an exotic Istanbul,
leaving on an ancient boat

Chapter 2

Two ads in the Personal Column of the Sunday Times elicited no response, so I decided to start off alone and hope to meet someone along the way. I had been trying to connect with others who might be travelling overland to India.

The idea of travelling alone was pretty daunting but, having no other option, I packed my small backpack, attached the rolled-up sleeping bag, and boarded the train for Istanbul on the first leg of the unplanned journey.

Far from being the intrepid explorer setting out to conquer exciting new lands, I felt small and timid and curled myself up on the seat, biting my nails and consoling myself that I could get off at the next stop, Munich, and return immediately should my courage fail me. Just before the train was due to start, however, the door of my compartment was flung open and a young guy threw himself and his backpack inside and slumped down on the opposite seat with his eyes closed, breathing heavily. Glancing at him – then, as his eyes were shut, looking more closely – I saw a bearded, long-haired individual about my own age. After a few deep breaths he sat up and opened his eyes and seemingly became aware of me for the first time. 'Nearly missed it,' he smiled ruefully.

He seemed quite nice so we chatted a little as the London suburbs gave way to country fields and the rain drizzled down. Finally he casually volunteered the information that he was on his way to India. I silently drew in a breath. Dare I ask to go with him? Quickly, before my courage failed, I said, 'Me too. Can I go with you?' Without hesitation he nodded his head – thank god for those easy, casual hippie days – and went on to say that actually he too was looking to meet with some other people because there was no doubt that the journey was fairly dangerous and strange things could happen if one was alone. In fact, he said, he was hoping to form a bigger group as this made sharing hotel rooms and train carriages cheaper and safer.

Wow! Ten minutes into the journey and I had a travelling companion! Problem sorted. Things were looking up. We slept through France and Switzerland but were awakened early the next morning by the noise and bustle of the Munich train station where our compartment door was opened and another young guy peered in. 'Can we sit here?' he asked, first in German and then in English. We nodded assent and two more guys appeared, complete with long hair and backpacks. Introductions all round identified our new companions as Hans, Dietrich and Pieter and my new English friend as Simon. My name then was Leisha. Having within minutes discovered that we were on the way to India, the Germans immediately suggested we band together saying that a group of six was an ideal number. Safety in numbers and all that. They were of the opinion that a pack of six was sufficient deterrent to possible dangers. One more person to go – and in the meantime I had acquired four bodyguards!

The three Germans were university students on their summer vacation and explained that they meant to travel fairly quickly as they only had two months' holiday. This suited me as I had a possible date in Delhi in about seven weeks' time. A few months previously I had met an American man, Alex, who had studied Asian Studies at Benares Hindi University in Benares. (The name of the city has now reverted to the Hindi name of Varanasi). Alex was a budding film maker and had made a successful short documentary on burial and cremation practices in Benares. Following this success, he had been commissioned by the Asian Studies department of his university in the USA to make four more documentaries about religious customs in India. I was superfluous to requirements at this point, and anyway he was flying to India with his small film crew and all the photographic equipment.

But I was not about to be left behind. Even if I did not in the end meet up with him, my appetite was whetted by visions of untravelled roads and exotic little-known countries. In London I had been enthralled by the stories of two friends who had just returned from a hazardous journey on the overland route to and from India. India had recently become popular due to the Beatles' visit to the Maharishi Mahesh Yogi's ashram in Rishikesh in 1968 (it was now 1971) and a few westerners were following in their footsteps, lured by visions of mysticism – or unlimited drugs with no policing.

I was intrigued by the prospect of journeying though far distant lands such as Turkey, Iran and Afghanistan, finally to end up in mystical India. And at the back of my mind there was a very small idea of going even further east to Japan, a country which I had been obsessed with since I was a teenager; a country which was, actually, of greater interest to me than India. But I had tentatively arranged to meet Alex in Delhi as he was passing through on a filming assignment, and I had no idea what would develop thereafter.

Good companions on this route overland were essential and I was very relieved to have met such nice people. Our train journey continued uneventfully from Germany though sundry eastern European countries, none of which were visible because it was night. We entered Bulgaria early the next morning – and the train stopped. Delays were inevitable, that we understood, but after four hours we started to get a bit impatient – but our enquiries yielded no information. We had tried to get out of the train to stretch our legs but were shouted at and even threatened by a uniformed guy holding a gun! We hurriedly re-embarked but soon another more amiable man arrived who told us we could walk beside the train as long as we didn't go more than ten feet away from it. We did not require a visa to travel through Bulgaria but did need one if we entered the country – which according to this guard legally began ten feet away from the train!

So we paraded up and down our ten-foot wide barren promenade and soon met two English girls doing the same thing. They were Mandy and Cecilia and were very beautiful. I could see the guys speculating on further female travelling companions and I would have loved to have some female friends, but unfortunately for us the girls were only going as far as Istanbul. They joined us in our carriage and it was good to have more friends as we were stuck in this grim, grey railway yard for the whole day. Finally we went to sleep and were dimly aware that the train had started sometime in the early hours of the morning.

This meant we entered Istanbul at sunrise. We awoke to religious cries from endless minarets exhorting the faithful to prayer and the rosy rays of the sun bathing the dome of Hagia Sophia – ex-church, ex-mosque, now famous museum – in pinks and oranges. It was surreal. We were stunned into silence at the glorious scene unfolding in front of us. This was our first taste of the East. What a beginning!

Practicalities soon surfaced, however. Having had almost no food for the past thirty-six hours we were extremely hungry and urgently needed showers. Mandy and Cecilia had booked themselves into a small guest house and I decided to join them. The guys disappeared to seek rougher digs. The little guest house was basic but clean and there was a room with three beds so we could share costs. Seeing the small attached bathroom we all had but one idea − shower! We immediately undressed and Mandy turned on the tap. No water! What? After a few minutes of fruitless effort, not a single drop materialised so we quickly put the clothes back on again and rushed out to reception to find out what the water story was. The receptionist spoke only a little English but cheerfully made us understand that there was no water in the city at this time. When? Shrugs of shoulders. Today? Tomorrow? No idea.

We stood there nonplussed. No possibility even of washing! Then I noticed a small stand with some little cards showing a picture of what seemed to be some public baths. The little grey cells connected in my brain − Turkish Baths? I showed the card to the receptionist and asked if we could go there. He shrugged again disinterestedly but indicated that it was a possibility if we wanted to try. We most certainly did, so we quickly went back to the room, grabbed shower necessities, clean clothes, passports and money and set off following the rough map shown on the back of the little card.

It wasn't far. We at first caused almost a riot by going into what we found out was the men's entrance but, after being loudly chastened by a yelling attendant and hastily backing out, we went round to a side entrance and were admitted by a fat old woman dressed all in black. She took us to some cubicles and forcefully mimed that we were to disrobe completely. Well, it seemed we had no choice so we obediently did as we were told, stripped naked and then followed her into the baths.

What then transpired I still count as one of the most beautiful travel experiences I have had in all my many years of travel around the planet.

Through a small door we entered a church-like structure of white marble. The building was in the shape of a cross with a domed central crossing and cupolas spanning each of the four arms of the cross. The end of each arm formed a semi-circle, ornamented with three carved basins which received torrents of water spewing out through the mouths of carved gargoyle-like creatures. The water continuously overflowed the basins and cascaded down three marble steps into the central area, ending in a square shallow pool underneath the central dome. As the water was comfortably hot, a faint steam arose which gave the whole scene a misty, ethereal quality. The most extraordinary feature was that the dome and cupolas were inset with little 'windows' of coloured glass in all colours of the rainbow. The sun shining through the coloured glass made shimmering, sparkling patterns of colour on the water cascading over the marble steps and floor into the central pool. It was simply breathtaking.

We were stunned into stillness but soon the now naked old woman came up to us and shooed us into one of the fountain areas and then gave us each two carved wooded stools and a wooden ladle. Still a bit dazed we sat on one stool, put our stuff on the other and slowly filled the ladles with water from the basins to pour over ourselves. When the old woman saw that we had understood the required cleansing procedures she left us alone. We then got on with the business of washing bodies and hair, laughing all the time. I felt we were like nymphs in an enchanted glade and imagined the scene we were creating – three young women, one with long black hair, one with long brown hair and one with long blonde hair, now glistening wet with the falling water, set against a background of white marble dotted at intervals with varied rippling shapes of colour from the glass in the roof. I remarked that I thought David Bailey or the like should be here to photograph the scene. Mandy and Cecelia laughingly agreed.

Once deliciously clean, we walked down to the shallow pool and lazed almost submerged in the soft warm water. On its surface now floated a few soap suds which again reflected the colours from the glass in the dome.

I think we stayed there about two hours, reluctant to leave such a magical place.

The hunger pangs disturbed, however, so we finally set off back to the guest house to deposit our shower stuff and then walked down a hill looking for the restaurant the guys had mentioned.

It must be remembered that at this time there was almost no organised tourism and there was absolutely nothing to guide us, especially not in English. Lonely Planet and Fodor's guides had not yet been conceived. We functioned on the ancient system of word-of-mouth – following tips passed on by the few people who had travelled this road before us. I had written down some information from my two friends in England and the Germans had their own collection of tips gleaned from people they knew. The restaurant mentioned had become a well-known contact point for foreign, low-budget travellers and everyone went there to meet and swap experiences and information. The food was known to be inexpensive and reasonably safe to eat.

We met the still grubby guys who also hadn't found water to wash in and I could see the appreciative looks in their eyes at our pristine cleanliness! We devoured the food put before us and then sat back to confer. We had agreed to spend a few days in Istanbul to see the famous landmarks before continuing eastwards. That afternoon we did little else than meander around the area (the guys disappeared off to find the Baths) and soon a proper bed beckoned. We had slept sitting up for the past three nights.

Awaking early the next morning before the other two girls, I slipped out of the room wanting to see Hagia Sophia in the soft, early morning light – and alone. I had studied this architectural wonder in my art classes in school and it had always seemed a place of extraordinary grace and beauty and I wanted to savour my impressions in silence. It did not disappoint. It was magnificent – softly lit by the early morning light and peaceful with only a few early morning visitors. How can I express its beauty and majesty? I can't. I will have to leave its praises unsung because only physically being there can be suffice to appreciate its uniqueness.

I finally made my way back to the meeting-point restaurant for some food and found Pieter and Simon there. Together we went off to see the other great architectural splendour of Istanbul, the Blue Mosque. It was everything it was made out to be and more. Again words fail me. All I can say is that we were transported into beautiful otherworldly spaces by the peaceful ambience of the place and the filtered blue light passing through the stained glass of the many windows.

After a nap back at the hotel I met Pieter and Simon again and we wandered down to the sea front, just soaking up the exotic atmosphere of the place. It was magical. Istanbul is one of the places I later vowed never to revisit. At that time it was its original self, untouched by the voracious tourism of our current decades. It would never be the same if I went there again and I don't want to spoil or supplant the exquisite memories I have of such a special place.

We came down to earth with a bit of a bump that evening,

however, when we again met at the restaurant. There we teamed up again with Hans and Dietrich who had in tow a very good-looking Italian named, predictably, Giovanni. He wanted to join us on the trip overland. As his presence would make up the desired number of six, we all quickly agreed. Giovanni was a medical student and very organised and efficient and he immediately asked what our next step on the road would be. We sort of blinked in bewilderment at him because none of us had actually thought that far yet.

He had a novel idea to offer. Instead of bus or train or hitchhiking he had heard that it was fairly easy to get a cheap cabin with six berths on a cargo boat that carried goods to the Black Sea, ending at a place called Trabzon. From there we could get a local bus to Erzurum, the largest city in eastern Turkey.

This actually sounded quite good and Giovanni undertook to investigate the situation the next morning and we would meet at lunchtime to hear the results of his research. He had already been in Istanbul for a week and wanted to be on the move.

The rest of us wanted at least one more day in Istanbul and I especially wanted to visit the Grand Bazaar which Mandy and Cecelia had heard about. Shopping was an urgent necessity.

OH MY GOD!! Retail heaven!! I was unprepared for this absolutely amazing place – only later learning that it was one of the largest and oldest covered markets in the world, having opened in 1461. It was great that the guys weren't with us as we three girls descended into a delicious shopping stupor, intrigued by anything and everything. Mandy and Cecelia could do full justice to the merchandise on offer as they were going straight back to England and could carry quite a lot of stuff but I had to restrain myself as I had only a small backpack. Of course we were immediate targets for the locals and shopkeepers as I think we were the only foreigners there. Certainly we didn't see another western European person during the whole five hours we spent there. But because there were three of us, we weren't pestered much and simply had the most glorious fun. I bought a beautiful embroidered cotton top – cream with peach-pink embroidery – and an embroidered waistcoat to wear in the Muslim countries I would soon be passing through. It was good to cover up as much as possible to avoid being hassled.

Now pretty tired after such a shopping marathon we decided that we still had to see the Topkapi Palace before I left to go further east and Mandy and Cecelia left to go for some sun and sea south of Istanbul for a few days. Topkapi was the one disappointment in Istanbul. Having seen the 1964 movie with Melina Mercouri and Peter Ustinov, I was expecting something more impressive. Instead it was quite tatty and unkempt and tourists were only allowed into one rather dowdy room with a precious dagger on view, and the very untidy garden.

So we didn't stay long and returned to the restaurant and chatted with other travellers until the guys arrived. Giovanni had amazing news. There was a boat leaving in the morning and he had booked us a cabin on it. This guy was quite something! Actually we were all now ready to move and so, after eating our last good meal for the next few days, we drifted back to our various beds. Early the next morning the guys picked me up and we set off down to the harbour. Mandy and Cecelia couldn't resist seeing this unusual departure so came with us to say their goodbyes.

The boat was old and rusty but the captain came out to

greet us and the rest of the crew were welcoming and friendly, so we decided this could be chalked up as one more interesting experience. We dumped our stuff in a scruffy little cabin and returned to the deck to wave good bye to the English girls and enjoy the receding spectre of this most wonderful of cities.

Istanbul to Mashhad, Iran – by boat, bus and train

one pleasant sea journey,
two nightmarish bus and train rides,
many gorgeous carpets and friendly people in Mashhad

Chapter 3

Our old tub glided sedately up the Bosphorus and we enjoyed the calm warm weather with the water reflecting a very blue sky. The two days and nights we spent on the ship were pleasant and uneventful although one brief period ashore in some strange harbour was a rather grim experience. I have no idea what the place was, must have been a cargo stop, but we found ourselves wandering between hundreds of ancient rusty steam engines. It looked like a graveyard for these old discarded machines! How on earth did they get there? I felt a few cold shivers as I realised this port was very much Soviet influenced and the prevailing feeling was dark and slightly menacing.

We finally docked in Trabzon, in north-eastern Turkey, an unusual and fascinating, almost quirky, city built on a narrow piece of land between the sea and mountains. Picturesque buildings clung to the mountainside which was lushly covered in green foliage. Trabzon was located on the historic Silk Road and has always been an important trading city. I loved its ambience and wished that I could have stayed longer; for me it evoked visions of the romance of travel and the interchange of cultures. But the guys weren't similarly impressed and wanted to push on. Close to the harbour they found a bus depot and got us tickets for a bus ride to the eastern Turkish city of Erzurum. Had I known what this bus journey was going to entail, I might have stood my ground and demanded a few days respite.

Perhaps it was just as well that we did not know what we were letting ourselves in for. That bus journey shares the dubious honour of being one of my top three most terrifying road trips I have experienced. The road from Kathmandu to the Chinese Tibetan border in Nepal comes in at number one and the old road from Bombay to Poona in India takes third place.

The bus was a typical local one, filled with peasants and their animals and sundry other weird personages. I had a window seat and, unfortunately, an excellent view of the scenic sights. No doubt the jagged mountain ranges and steep valleys covered in evergreen trees were spectacular, but the fact that we were hurtling down a rubble-strewn dirt road more or less the exact width of the bus with a sheer drop on the window side, robbed me of any enjoyment of the views. It seemed to me that the bus even sometimes tilted over when the wheels appeared to lose traction and the bus teetered on the edge. Nightfall heightened the fears as an extraordinarily bright full moon rose, revealing further stunning vistas, but all I could focus on was the question of whether or not the driver could actually even see where he was going. Needless to say it was a sleepless night for all – my frightened whimpers and muffled shrieks must have affected my poor travel mates – and when we finally staggered out of the bus in Erzurum we felt pretty wrecked by the ordeal.

All but Giovanni…. Displaying again his future doctor's temperament of coolness and togetherness in times of emergency, he marshalled us together and announced that another bus ride onwards was not acceptable and the next journey should be by train. We were in total agreement and set off for the train station. It transpired that there was a through train all the way to Tehran leaving that evening so we bought the tickets and optimistically booked six berths in a compartment.

Erzurum was disappointing after Trabzon and revealed nothing of interest so we had some food in a restaurant and then in a local market, anticipating a long, less-than-luxurious train journey, bought a whole lot more strange edibles and bottles of drinking water to last us on the fourteen hour journey ahead. Despite these preparations being adequately achieved, I noticed Giovanni still looking around searching for something. Finally I heard him grunt in approval as he found a small kiosk selling wooden objects, among them some walking sticks. We watched with curiosity as he haggled with the vendor over a particularly stout looking stick and when the transaction was finished we gathered round to ask him what this was for. He just laughed and told us to wait and see.

Knowing that being first in a queue was paramount we decided to hang out at the train station and board the train as soon as we were allowed, if not before. Often as foreigners we got away with behaviour that would not be accepted from locals! We simply got on the train, surprisingly found our compartment and sat down with relief. All but Giovanni.... As soon as the last person was in he slammed the door and jammed the walking stick under the handle and then piled his backpack on top of the stick. Then he asked us for towels or jackets and made piles of our luggage against the compartment windows, thus preventing anyone from being able to look in. At the same time he told us to close the shutters on the windows on the platform side and to hang whatever we could over any possible places that someone could look through. Only when we had finally barricaded ourselves in and were sitting in semi-darkness and stifling heat did he relax, look around and grin widely at our surprised faces.

He then told us that in Istanbul he had met some people returning from Afghanistan who had forewarned him about this train journey. Apparently it would become very crowded and the locals would take over any unprotected compartment, crowding at least twenty or thirty people into a space suitable for six. He told us to be ready for assaults on our space. He was very soon proved right and the door and windows were repeatedly battered, the blows being accompanied by loud yells and angry threats. But the stick held firm and the attacks decreased once the train started to move.

Well, we were safe for a while but after a few hours a pee break became an urgent necessity. The toilet excursion was planned with military precision. Speed was of the utmost. At the count of three, Pieter jerked the stick from under the handle, Giovanni and Simon shot out one to each side of the door and Hans quickly moved out between them. Pieter then slammed the door shut and replaced the stick.

We waited in a silence disturbed by renewed assaults and shouts. I must admit I was really scared by now because the further east we went, the more violent the men seemed to get, and we had heard many stories of young western women getting attacked. I had covered myself from neck to feet and at all times wore a skirt, not jeans or trousers, but now I even wrapped a scarf of Pieter's around my hair and lower part of my face to imitate the dress mode of the local women.

When the three guys returned we reversed the strategy but they still had to use force to prevent the other passengers trying to get into the compartment. We waited another hour before making the next toilet excursion with the remaining three. Fortunately it was now dark and people had quietened down, no doubt getting ready for sleep. We repeated the manoeuvre, this time with me in the middle. People were sleeping in the corridor so we had to step over them, but fortunately they didn't hassle us as much as earlier and we were able to complete the proceedings with less trouble. On regrouping the guys decided that in an emergency they could use a bottle and empty it out of the window, thus necessitating an excursion only for my needs! I didn't drink anything after that.

Finally, early the next morning, we stopped on the outskirts of Tabriz in Iran where a group of swarthy unpleasant-looking immigration officials boarded the train to check passports. Our papers were all in order but we heaved a sigh of relief when the train pulled into the station in Tabriz. Surprisingly a lot of people got off the train and not so many got on, so the remaining few hours to Tehran were relatively uneventful.

We were all in accord that we did not want to stop in Tehran; the hippie grapevine had related nothing but horror stories about the place and its inhabitants. Certainly they looked a menacing lot as we stepped off the train into the station. The women were mostly covered in long full-length black veils with only their eyes showing and they never looked ahead, only focussing on the ground in front of them. Very, very uncomfortable.

The grapevine had provided the information that the bus station was just outside the train station and that buses left fairly frequently to Mashhad, our next stop only about two or three hours away. We changed money at a little office and then easily found the bus station where we got tickets for a bus leaving in about two hours which would get us to Mashhad in the late afternoon. In the meantime what to do?

Having had no sleep the previous night and very little the last night, we were tired and hot and dirty. A coffee place was conveniently situated close by and we sat down to have a few shots of the strong stuff – still very much what one would call 'Turkish' coffee. Simon wandered off looking for a toilet and came back after a few minutes saying that he had discovered what appeared to be public baths. We all perked up at that and grabbed our gear and followed him. Yes, these were public baths but no, females were not allowed. The attendant was adamant. I cannot say how much I was longing for a bath or shower because on the boat there had been only a tap so the last real cleanse was back in Istanbul about five days previously.

I decided to plead with some money placed on the counter. A heated discussion followed with neither me nor the attendant understanding a word but I kept on adding notes to the pile. The protestations faltered and my smile widened winningly until finally there was a change. Looking left and right he beckoned us all in, sent the guys off in one direction and took me in another. I felt a quick shiver of fear and slowed a bit but he flung open a door and gestured me to go inside. There was so much steam I could hardly see anything but it seemed to be a small empty room and there was definitely the sound of running water somewhere. The attendant closed the door after me and I could see there was a kind of bolt with which I immediately locked the door.

This was a far cry from the magical place in Istanbul! It was a small concrete room with a concrete bench to sit on, a drain running the length of the room and a single dim light set into the wall. It was more like a sauna, hot and full of steam. But there was an actual shower! Wunderbar! Fifteen minutes later I was almost fainting from lack of oxygen but was beautifully clean again. Only when you have been dirty for so long can you really appreciate what it is like to be clean, even if your clothes are still rather grubby. Having got myself and gear together, I was wondering what I should do next when there was a loud hammering on the door. I cautiously opened it to the attendant outside gesturing impatiently for me to follow him. I did and was soon outside and the guys joined me within a few minutes. It seemed like one was only allowed to be there for fifteen or twenty minutes as the attendant had been to fetch them too. I glanced back at him and gave him a little bow and he actually smiled! First smile we had seen since we left the boat in Trabzon, I think. I will never know if it was the money and my feminine wiles that got me an illegal shower or if there actually was a facility for women and the attendant's protests were only an attempt to try for a bribe.

I don't remember the journey to Mashhad except that it was a reasonably comfortable bus on a reasonable road, almost a highway. I think we were probably all asleep. Looking back I am aware there are often big gaps in my memory of a place and conclude that this is because I was asleep or it was night so I didn't see anything while we were travelling.

Mashhad was fabulous! After the terror of the mountain bus ride, the potential violence of the train ride and the grimness and hostility of Tehran, Mashhad was a delight. It was high on a hill with rather beautiful buildings and wide streets and the people seemed to be relaxed and smiling. Even the women, despite their veils, were happily chatting away and looked at us with openness and great curiosity. And soon we saw some foreigners, German hippies, who were happy to see us. They had been in the city for a few days and said there were quite a few travellers there who were more or less welcomed with no hassles. They told us of a possible place to stay so off we went to investigate.

Fortune was smiling. We had a feeling of hitting the jackpot as we were greeted by a very pleasant man who, on seeing me, called his wife who appeared delighted to see a foreign woman. She actually clapped her hands in delight. Bless! They took us upstairs to the rooftop – all the houses had flat roofs – which they had creatively turned into a spotlessly clean guestroom with four beds and dividing trellises intertwined with climbing plants and brightly coloured flowers. There were palm trees in pots and grass mats on the floor. But only four beds? As if reading our thoughts they indicated that they could add an extra bed and then the wife beckoned to me with a mischievous little smile. She took me down to the second floor and showed me a tiny white room with a bed and a chair and a plant and a view over the back garden. A luxury room in a Hilton Hotel would not have made me more ecstatic. Just to be on my own for a night or two would be absolute bliss.

They didn't serve food but the charming man took us around the corner to a small restaurant which ended up being our dining room for the rest of our stay as the food was the best we had eaten on our trip so far – simple, plain and healthy. And cheap.

We were very tired and went early to bed after quickly agreeing that we would stay here for at least two nights.

In the end we stayed for three nights because we needed a rest and to take things easy and Mashhad was such a great place to hang out in. We made friends with other travellers and enjoyed having space from each other. It was amazing that during the whole, at times quite tense, journey we as a group had actually experienced no disharmony but easily flowed into whatever situations presented themselves. Quite extraordinary as we had only met about ten days before.

But, a little separation was good. I met a Danish couple and Elsa, the girl, obviously needed some space from her partner too, so we took off on our own to shop and explore together while her man happily went in a different direction with Simon.

Mashhad! Carpets, carpets, carpets.... Everywhere. In glorious rich hues. And turquoise stones being peddled on every corner. Beautiful mosques. And wonderful bazaars. Strangely, two women alone were not hassled so we felt quite free to wander around. There was an ancient, apparently important library. People were friendly and a few tried to speak English to us -- which was fun and worth a considerable number of cups of coffee. There was a lot of fruit to eat, melons in particular.

Looking at photos on the internet of Mashhad today I almost don't recognise it. And I think again how lucky I was to travel at that time because so much of the special ambience of places like this has vanished forever.

At the end of the second day we had a short conference in our dining room and agreed that, much as we loved this city and our spectacular accommodation, we should be moving on the next day as there was still the whole of Afghanistan to explore, then Pakistan and finally India, our ultimate destination.

The next morning, after effusive goodbyes to our kind and charming hosts, we caught a bus for Taibad from where we would cross the border into Afghanistan.

Well, that was the plan....

Mashhad to Herat – by bus

a dangerous mission, drugs at the border,
jails and various authorities

Chapter 4

Having been cushioned by the very pleasant and relaxed atmosphere of Mashhad, it was a rude awakening to be confronted with the underlying hostility of the regular Iranian people and the harsh, bleak environment in which they lived. After an hour on the bus I was thinking, 'Get me out of here!' and was looking forward to being in Afghanistan of which we had heard many good reports.

Finally, about midday we reached Taibad, the border town from where we would cross into Afghanistan. As we alighted from the bus, however, we heard angry shouts and saw three uniformed Iranians dragging a yelling German guy towards what looked like a guard house. About twelve westerners were milling around looking shocked and frightened. Pieter asked some people what was going on. The man he first spoke to sullenly turned away but someone else said that the guards had found a kilo of hashish in the bag of the guy we saw being dragged away. Pieter told us that this man was shouting that he had not been smuggling dope but that the hashish had been put into his bag by someone else.

We digested this information in silence. This was of course a popular excuse when illegal drugs were found but it was also a well-known fact that unscrupulous people did slip drugs into other peoples' baggage just before crossing a border and then try to get it back on the other side, usually offering money to the innocent courier. We had been warned of this and told to watch our luggage at all times and were glad that we had already established a bit of a routine around this issue.

It turned out that the sullen man we had first talked to was the apparent friend of the German guy who had been arrested so Pieter, Hans and Dietrich tried to question him more. There had been many frightening stories of westerners being, rightly or wrongly, arrested and thrown into Middle Eastern jails without anybody knowing where they were, so no help could be provided. There were stories of westerners having horrific experiences of being locked away and dying because authorities failed to tell anybody about their situation.

This man disturbed us and I think it was uppermost in the minds of many of the onlookers that it was actually he who had slipped the drugs into his companion's luggage.

Pieter, Hans and Dietrich translated what they had been talking about to Simon, Giovanni and me and said that they wanted to talk to the guy who had been arrested to see if we could help. So we walked over to the small guard house where he had been locked up. There was a barred window through which we could see and talk to him. I will call him Johan. He told us that he didn't really know the man with whom he had been travelling but asked us to tell him to inform the German Embassy and his parents where he was and to try to get help for him. He was trying to give us his parents' address when some guards saw us and started running towards us. We stood our ground but they grabbed the guys and started dragging them away from the window. As a female, I was the last to be approached so I quickly tried to memorise Johan's particulars; he was fortunately able to switch into English so I could understand better. Finally I left too as I realised I was about to be accosted and we quickly regrouped and wrote down the information Johan had given.

Pieter gave the piece of paper to the so-called friend who grudgingly took it and said he would inform the German authorities when he was able to. With that we had to be content.

We discovered that the bus for Herat only left in the evening so had an uncomfortable few hours sitting under a scraggly tree whiling away the hot afternoon. The surrounds were desolate – a bleak dry desert – and the other travellers were tired and dispirited. Finally an old rickety bus arrived and we put our luggage on the roof as instructed and crammed inside along with the usual locals and their goods and chattels and chickens and goats etc. All seats were occupied so it looked like we would have to stand for the whole three-hour journey unless some people got out along the way. In fact we had driven only about a mile out of the town when the bus broke down. The driver ordered us all out and we sat on the side of the road, still disturbed by the ugly scenes we had witnessed that day. I was uneasy because I did not trust that man to get help for Johan. If it really was he who had tried to smuggle the drugs, there was no way he was going to go anywhere near someone in authority in case he drew suspicions towards himself.

Then Simon, who was also silent, turned to me and asked, 'Are you thinking what I am thinking?' I asked him what he was thinking and yes, he also had no confidence that that man would report to relevant authorities. We all joined in the discussion and finally both Pieter and Simon said they felt tha they should do something – like return to Mashhad and find the German Embassy or Consulate and report the incident. We pooled our brains to remember the details Johan had given us about his parents.

For the first time on our trip, however, we were not in

agreement. Giovanni, Hans and Dietrich had been planning to leave Pieter, Simon and myself in Herat because they wanted to go into the far northern areas of Afghanistan and Pakistan looking for signs of the lost tribes of Israel. It was thought that the Pashtun people were descendants of these tribes and a few clues existed to prove the point: many people in that area had blue eyes, names resembled Jewish names and there were remnants of customs and practices similar to those in Jewish traditions. At that time few westerners had explored these regions and it was really wild and dangerous.

After some discussion we sadly decided that our paths would now finally diverge. Giovanni, Hans and Dietrich would continue and Pieter, Simon and I would return to Mashhad, find the German Consul and report Johan's situation. I had an address of a person in Delhi which Alex, my American friend, had given me as a way of contacting him and I gave it to our three friends in the hope that, if we made it to Delhi at a similar time, we could meet up again.

Then Pieter, Simon and I got the bags off the top of the bus, necessitating much reorganisation up there which brought forth angry shouts and shaking fists from the bus driver who was still trying to get the engine sorted out. We trudged back the mile or so on the desert road in the dark, hoping to meet with no further hassles. When we got back it was about 8.30pm and we found that providentially there was a bus going back to Mashhad in about twenty minutes time. After buying the tickets we decided to see if we could reach Johan's little jail and tell him what we planned to do. It might help to calm his mind and give him some hope and peace. We also thought that it would be helpful if we could get the number of his passport.

The gate to the small compound was now locked but we

could see a guard sitting and smoking a little way inside. Simon quickly suggested that I play a sorrowing female game and try to persuade the guard to open the gate. I would be less of a threat. Hmmnnn.... Slightly worried about my own safety because these Iranian men were not my idea of chivalrous manhood, I agreed to try, and even managed to shed a few bogus tears as I begged to see my friend. The guard was a bit bewildered but I guess he was facing a long boring night and this was a diversion so he actually let me in. I was able to tell Johan what we were going to do, to see the relief on his face and to get the place of issue of his passport and its first three numbers before the guard had second thoughts and roughly grabbed my arm and pushed me back through the gate. But mission had been mostly accomplished.

We got back on the bus and dozed all the way to Mashhad, arriving there at about 11pm. We had decided to go back to our kind hosts and see if we could stay there again if they had not already let the beds out to someone else. Because of the time we had spent with them we knew that they were awake until fairly late so we hoped we would not disturb them too much.

The town was almost deserted and only sparsely lit so we were a bit uneasy now that we were only three instead of six. Our fears were justified. After a few minutes two big Iranian guys started to follow us. Pieter and Simon, both slight men, would be no match for them and I wouldn't stand any chance at all! What these men were after, me or money, was not clear but for the first time ever I experienced an existential understanding of the expression 'fear giving one wings'! We flew down the street despite being encumbered by the backpacks -- only to find our host's house in darkness and the door firmly closed. By now Pieter and Simon were fighting off the two Iranians so it was me banging on the door and screaming to be let in. Suddenly I saw a bell in the top corner so I held my finger on it until, wonderfully, I heard noises inside and the door being unbolted. When the kind man opened it I shot inside and ran upstairs as quickly as I could, deciding it was up to the men to sort things out. It didn't take long! Only a few minutes later Pieter and Simon arrived with our host all laughing, albeit a bit shakily, at the incident. The guys told me that our host was magnificent and had roared at the two Iranians who quickly turned tail and slunk away in the face of one of their own kind taking them to task. Luckily there were no other guests and we were able to spend the night there.

Unfortunately being unable to communicate with our hosts, we set off into town the next morning wondering how we were going to find a German Consul or something similar. I had a vague recollection of seeing a sign saying 'British Council' somewhere and was eventually able to track down the place. British Council offices exist in many countries in the world to further good relations and cultural exchanges between Britain and the relevant country.

Again fortune smiled. We were shown into the office of a very nice man called Ken to whom we told our story. He was very reassuring, telling us that, although there was no German Consul in the town, he was used to dealing with these not uncommon events and would take responsibility for Johan. He was pleased when we gave him the details of Johan's parents and the incomplete passport details, saying that this kind of information was very helpful. He then explained that Johan would be brought from Taibad to Mashhad and put into a jail here where he would face some kind of court. Ken, as the only foreign person of authority in the town, would be informed of this and he would immediately take charge of the case. He said he was already overseeing the cases of two other foreigners currently in jail and also said that a kilo of hashish was a comparatively insignificant amount and he thought that Johan would be sent home to Germany within a few months. We were hugely relieved.

Ken went a step further by phoning the German Consul in Tehran immediately and we heard him pass over all the details. He said that Johan's parents would be immediately contacted.

We were noticeably sagging with relief and the final touch to our successful mission was to be given a fantastic cup of English tea which, in lieu of all we had been through, tasted like the proverbial nectar.

After taking leave of this wonderful man we went to the market and bought loads of fruit and sweets and whatever delicacies we could find to take back as presents to our saviours at the guest house. This time it was even hugs all round as we said our second goodbyes and went off to the bus station. Once on the bus I mentioned to Pieter, who I was sitting next to, that I wished we could tell Johan that he was being taken care of. Imagine our surprise when, at some small town on the way, the bus stopped and a guard and a hand-cuffed Johan boarded the bus!

There were two empty seats in front of us and we stood up and excitedly waved to Johan to come and sit there. He did, with the guard next to him, but when I started to tell him what had transpired the guard suddenly turned round and hit me across my face! I was totally shocked but we didn't want to protest in case Johan was affected. Then Pieter turned to me and started to talk in German. Understanding a little, I quickly realised he was telling the story of what we had managed to do so that Johan could hear all the details and be reassured. It worked, because when we got out at Taibad, Johan flashed a grateful smile at us and tossed a ring at me before being hauled off the bus. He must have worked the ring off his finger when the guard wasn't looking. I was so touched and wore that ring for many months.

We caught a bus within an hour to continue our journey to the now very much longed-for Afghanistan.

Herat to Bamiyan – by local transport
the best experience on the whole journey – by far

Chapter 5

Afghanistan as it was then, summer 1971, still tops my list as the most awesome country I have been to – for many reasons. It was raw, wild, formidable; the rugged scenery was breathtakingly magnificent and the people, although mostly poor, were noble, dignified, fierce, charming and extraordinarily good-looking.

What has happened since I travelled in Afghanistan is a tragedy of the highest order. Since 1978, when the Soviet Union began a ten year war, many hundreds of thousands of Afghan civilians have been killed or have fled as refugees to other countries. The country suffers from ongoing internal conflict and instability – the civil war from 1992 to 1996, the rise and fall of the Taliban government and the current unrest beginning in 2001 – and its economy and infrastructure are in ruins.

And yet, from the huge visual media coverage – news items, documentaries, YouTube videos and photographs – one can catch glimpses of the awesome place it once was. I dare not speculate if it can ever regain some of that splendour.

In this chapter perhaps I can convey something of what I, and others, of course, experienced while travelling its little-known paths.

* * *

Between the Iranian and Afghani borders there was a stretch of barren 'no-man's land' for about six miles. We had assumed that we would enter Afghanistan by late afternoon and make it to Herat by the evening. Wrong assumption. Hippie travellers were of course going to be targeted by the locals, and their comical assault began by delaying the bus's arrival at the border post. We (there must have been eleven or twelve westerners, about five of them female) sat unmoving for at least two hours in that 'no-man's land' until just before 5pm when the bus started up again and stopped at the immigration control. We were all shepherded out of the bus and some rather charming uniformed officials – I certainly didn't feel threatened – relieved us of our passports with smiles of equal sweetness and guile. Telling us we could collect all the passports in the morning, they then disappeared, closing and locking the office doors behind them.

We were definitely a bit worried – although the bus driver seemed to be assuring us that all was OK – until the same officials reappeared from a back door dressed in the typical civilian clothes of colourful turbans, baggy pants and long jackets and cheerfully invited us to sit down with them. Other men joined and proceedings took on a surreal party-like atmosphere. Food was produced and offered and then the real reason for the charade was revealed: out came the hashish, free samples were dispersed and prices named. We could only smile ruefully, realising that we were totally trapped, sitting ducks at these guys' mercy, and had no option but to submit to this initiation rite.

Most of my fellow travellers were not averse to a smoke or two of the dope offered, but we were also aware that we were carrying all our money on us (usually in purses around our necks or waists) and we were in a strange country amongst strangers and so needed to stay alert and not succumb to too much temptation. In the end I don't think we were in any danger. It seemed the event was more like the western equivalent of dropping in at the local pub and having a beer and a bit of a socialise before going home! One or two of the men had learnt a smattering of English and so we had a few exchanges and lots of laughs and within a short space of time they quietly disappeared leaving us rather bemused and certainly on quite a high. One of the officials had genially indicated a sort of garden where we could sleep until morning so we unrolled our sleeping bags and laid them out in a line against the garden wall, rather like in a school dormitory. It was reasonably warm and the moonless desert sky was densely packed with bright brilliant stars undoubtedly enhanced by substances recently inhaled.

I dozed rather than slept and we were all up early. There were some toilets, none too clean but useable – but no water nor any kind of washing facility. Soon vendors arrived offering fruit and bread and other strange edibles and the immigration officials showed up at 7am. After the hostility and menace of the Iranians it was surprising and very heart-warming to find that everyone here was cheerful, relaxed and full of smiles and a grinning official handed out our passports, enjoying trying to match the photographs to the people! Without asking we were escorted to the local bus station where we boarded a ramshackle bus for Herat and were given warm farewell waves as we departed.

That was quite a reception. Never again was I to have such a welcome committee greet me with such charm and good will on entry to any country. We reached Herat after a comparatively short journey and found a room for the huge sum of about ten pence each in what, I suppose, was a kind of guest house. It was just a room with nothing in it except a a built-in brick stove − for winter months, I assumed − and in a passage a primitive washing place with basic toilet facilities.

I loved Herat! It was a sleepy kind of place with plain buildings, wide streets and horse-drawn vehicles. The only strange thing was you couldn't see any women because they were all covered from head to foot in the typical burkas. But from the body language you could see that the women were curious about us and I tried to see through the embroidered lattice-like opening in front of their eyes and convey some kind of greeting. I sensed equal curiosity from their side about me although they shied away from Pieter and Simon.

There was colour everywhere. And soft subtle colours, not the bright glaring colours we were later to see in Pakistan and India. The Afghanis favoured shades of olive green, subtle hues of blue and rich dark maroons. Everywhere we looked there were market stalls selling colourful bags and garments, many of which, I later found out, were made by the wandering nomadic tribes which criss-crossed the country on camels.

Within a few hours we were approached by a very good-looking young man who spoke surprisingly good English. He asked if he could practice his English on us and we quickly agreed because this gave us a chance to know what was going on with these intriguing people. His name was something that sounded like Ahman. He was seventeen years old and wanted to be an engineer. Being with him was amazing because wherever we went − and he was an adept tour guide − we were quickly surrounded by people who wanted to know all about us and took the chance to use his translating skills. Before leaving us he invited us to tea the next afternoon in the grounds of a mosque on the outskirts of the town.

This meeting with Ahman was to provide yet one more

unforgettable experience in my many years of travelling around the world.

The next day, in the mid-afternoon, Pieter, Simon and I found our way to the mosque, guided by its four pillars which could be seen rising above the low buildings of the town. A deep blue cloudless sky and the yellow-brown desert formed the backdrop to the white and blue decorated minarets and domed structure of the mosque. The square inner courtyard was filled with curiously contorted palm trees which made us feel we were in a surreal fantasy garden, with an Alice-in-Wonderland kind of quality. The place was dead silent and there was nobody there.

We waited awhile for our young friend to materialise but finally decided we must have misunderstood or something and turned to leave. But we were stopped by a shout and turned to see Ahman appear from behind the mosque, gesturing us to come and join him. We followed him round the back of the building and were faced with a picturesque scene.

On the fine yellow sand, amongst the mis-shapen palm trees and some bushes covered in dark pink flowers, he had laid a gorgeous, thick, richly-coloured silk carpet scattered with coloured silk cushions. At one end of the carpet there was a big gleaming copper samovar for boiling water and in front of it was a tray of beautiful glasses for the tea and some plates of food. Two men, dressed in subtly coloured traditional garb, stood to greet us. We all sat down on the cushions and one of the men, our young friend's uncle, I think, brewed the strong sweet tea and offered us little cakes to eat. For an hour we sat there chatting, drinking tea and just absorbing the extraordinary scene.

We weren't sure of Afghani protocol but after a while we

decided that we should perhaps indicate it was time to go as we didn't want to take up too much of their time. But it seemed we had made a good impression because, after a quick conference with the other two men, Ahman turned to us and said he and his family would like to invite us to their evening meal a few hours hence. We were very touched and of course agreed. After Ahman arranged to pick us up at our guest house, we expressed our profound thanks for this beautiful experience and slowly walked back into town to our small hotel room.

As I walked, it struck me again how lucky I had been to find such great travelling companions in Simon and Pieter, and indeed in my other sorely missed friends now in the far north of this country. They were all intelligent, sensitive and interested in everything and everybody. They were also incredibly relaxed and easy-going so we had practically no disagreements about either personal idiosyncrasies or travel plans. There are various theories that there cannot be successful platonic friendships between men and women but I beg to disagree. This was an example right here.

Best of all, these guys were not into drugs as so many of the people that we met were. Observing the latter travelers, I felt that drugs lessened rather than heightened awareness and when trying to communicate with people on drugs I had the feeling that their real selves were obscured by a haze. It was like trying to communicate with someone with a thick cloud in the way.

My friends added so much to the joys of travelling and all the experiences we had and all the people, especially the indigenous ones that we met.

That evening proved to be another very special experience – especially for me. We were greeted warmly by the male

members of Ahman's family and served the usual tea by
women who were not wearing a burkha now but still had
veils across their faces and tent-like garments covering their
bodies. There was a lot of quite loving communication going
on between all the family members and I got the feeling that,
although the women were hidden from general view, they
were appreciated and respected rather than being
downtrodden and abused. But I was the only women sitting
down to eat. We all sat on cushions and carpets on the floor
and were served by the women. I can't say the food was that
great – just a kind of stew which was eaten with the fingers
and lots of what I later discovered was called naan, a flat
bread covered in oil and garlic.

After the meal I could see Ahman having a discussion
with one of the woman. He then got up and brought her
round to me and introduced her as his mother. He asked me if
I would come with them both to the woman's part of the
house to meet the rest of the female family members. I was
delighted of course and, with all the men nodding genially, I
left the room and followed Ahman and his mother upstairs
and into a very big room with arched windows from which
the desert was just visible in the dusk.

For the first time I saw the faces of Afghani women! And
what beautiful, intelligent faces they were. There were six
women: grandmother, mother, two aunts and two teenage
sisters. I was faced with a barrage of questions – they weren't
at all shy – which Ahman translated. Of course the first
questions were if I was married and did I have children but
we soon moved on to my travels and what I thought of their
country. I told them that I found it strange not to see their
faces when I walked around and they all agreed, Ahman
included, that they did not like the system of burkas. This was

obviously a fairly well-educated and progressive family and Ahman said that none of the male family members liked hiding the women members but that they had to do it because the consequences were severe. If a woman dared to show her face in public she and her family could be prosecuted, ostracised or even, in a worst case scenario, stoned.

I felt sad for these women and hoped that their situation would improve as the years went by. In a way their situation has improved in that they now have greater freedom to be educated and not wear the burkha always, but this slight progress has been a bitter victory in the light of the recent horrific events in their country.

The meeting with Ahman and his family was the highlight of our week in the fascinating town of Herat but soon it was time to move on.

We caught a night bus to Kabul, stopping only for a few hours around midnight in what I think was Helmand Province where we met some interested local inhabitants and rested for a while on the sand just gazing at the breathtaking starry panorama that the desert sky, sans any form of artificial light, presented. When I watch or read of the ongoing battles now centred in this very area, I remember that night and am saddened at what is now happening. The only consolation is that perhaps this starry vista gives our soldiers some occasional respite amid the grimness of their daily battles.

* * *

Kabul was nothing special except that there were a lot more western travellers to talk to and some quite decent restaurants. But our goal was not to hang out in the comparative civilisation of the town but to journey into the mountains north west of there to visit the small village of

Bamiyan which we had heard a lot about. Another night journey in a much older, very dilapidated bus, jammed in between locals, goats, dogs, chickens and other paraphernalia gave us an unexpected glimpse of another facet of Afghanistan – the nomadic Kuchis.

Labouring up a narrow mountainous dirt road the bus pulled over and came to a stop. The stars were so bright that we could see a little of the road and hillside but the view through the window was suddenly obscured by what seemed to be a camel walking by. Then another followed. Experience dictated that any stop was a potential pee break and as a few of the other passengers started to get out of the bus, we followed.

Stepping down from the bus we immediately found ourselves in the middle of a convoy of camels, goats, sheep, donkeys and horses bearing huge loads of luggage – which we later found out were the tents and sundry goods and chattels belonging to the Kuchi nomads who constantly travelled the land. Some people were sitting on the camels but most seemed to be walking. They were, however dead silent except for the movement of the animals and I can't begin to describe what an eerie surreal experience it was to watch these ghostly apparitions as they passed by, looking neither left nor right. It took almost half an hour for the convoy to pass. I had heard of these nomads and hoped dearly for another chance to see them more closely and in daylight.

As the sun rose the next morning the bus stopped at a tea shop which was no more than a big tent obviously made from animal hides and we stiffly descended and drank some of the hot tea, so strong it gave a welcome jolt to the system. Like most of the other tea places we had been to, the routine involved taking off your shoes and climbing onto a high platform covered with carpets in rich colours. This time the novelty was that there were two women serving and they wore different, almost gypsy-like, clothes with no burkas. There were a few women in the bus with us and at this stop they removed their burkas too. Perhaps so far from civilisation they had no fear of prosecution. I was happy to see their strong-featured faces revealed and immediately tried to greet them with my one Afghani word of 'hello'.

In all my meetings with the Afghani people I was always struck by what I can only call 'their nobleness'. They would look one straight in the eye with neither fear nor obsequiousness and give a grave acknowledgement of your presence without being overtly friendly. I loved this demeanour.

The women serving tea were no different; they responded to my overtures with a kind of noble grace but kept their distance. Attempts to beg or gain from me were never made – so different to the ignoble Pakistanis and Indians I was later to meet.

We noticed a few men climbing on to the roof of the bus and thought this would be a great idea as we did not have much of a view of the country crammed inside. I felt a bit like I was riding on the prow of a ship as I sat up there with a now unrestricted view of the rugged terrain.

After a few hours we started to descend into a valley and soon green trees and shrubs coloured the view. We knew we were approaching Bamiyan which was an important stop on the ancient silk route because of the presence of water. Very soon we saw what we had come to see: the Bamiyan Buddhas, carved into the face of cliffs.

As early as the second century, Bamiyan had been a Buddhist religious site and monks lived in caves carved into the side of the cliffs. In the sixth and seventh centuries two giant statues of Buddha were carved into the same cliffs and, until they were blown up by the Taliban in 2001, were the largest statues of Buddha in the world.

I said at the beginning of this chapter that Afghanistan was probably the most awesome place I have visited on the planet. I just have to resort to superlatives and repetition when describing my journey! The sight of those Buddhas was simply extraordinary. Their grandeur, their size, their position, their age and the history that they represented was almost too much to take in. We stood dumbfounded and humbled at such splendour and enormous antiquity.

The deliberate destruction by the Taliban of the statues in 2001 must count as one of the greatest cultural crimes in the history of humanity. The statues profoundly affected me so I was devastated when I heard of this horrendous act.

Bamiyan at that time saw only a few western hippies so there was no accommodation available except in the homes of private families. We had been told that once we arrived the locals would come up to us and offer rooms in their houses – and this was indeed the case. After only a few minutes of getting off the bus a man came up to us and said, 'Room?' and grinned with pride at his English proficiency! When we nodded in agreement he took us to his house which was almost in the centre of the small settlement. Bamiyan at this time was just a large village, certainly not a town.

The man introduced himself as Sikkendoah (my spelling). Perhaps he was an important man in the village because he lived in a comparatively large compound consisting of a big house, built of mud and clay, with a walled garden. He was definitely the best-looking Afghani we had met – and most of them were very good-looking! His wife had a veil over the lower half of her face but her grey-green eyes were beautiful and the two young children were gorgeous. Prices were negotiated and we sat down to the inevitable cup of tea, pleased to be welcomed by genial people and housed in relative comfort. They didn't seem to find it strange that we were two men and one woman in a room. I guess they had already accepted western hippie ways.

After tea, Sikkendoah took us outside to proudly show us his garden which must have been about forty by forty metres. It only took us only a few seconds to realise that his whole crop was hemp i.e. hashish or cannabis! We had to grin at his obvious delight at our surprise but I thought he was going to be disappointed in that he had unusually hosted some people who were not much into his carefully-tended plants and its products. We indicated that later would be a better time to discuss this as our overriding desire was not to get stoned but to get closer to the Buddhas.

He helpfully guided us to the feet of the biggest Buddha, showed us an opening with some stairs on the side and started climbing. It was amazing! The stairs led up to different levels which were like landings with caves forming rooms leading off them. Only much later did I learn that Buddhist monks had lived here for centuries.

Finally we came out onto a landing level with the shoulder of the Buddha. A plank reaching from the landing to the shoulder had been laid and Sikkendoah nimbly crossed it and held out his hand to help us. Within seconds we were standing on the shoulder of the Buddha, holding on to his ear, and surveying the whole valley and the mountains beyond.

After sitting silently there for about an hour we realised we were pretty tired and hungry and so returned to our new lodgings to have a nap. This room was also unfurnished so again our beds were our sleeping bags with the backpacks for pillows. After a walk in the evening, enjoying the views of the Buddhas and sitting next to a small lake which provided the water for the area as there was no river, we returned to the house where Sikkendoah was insistent that we partake of his garden wares. A few puffs was more than enough – the stuff was pure and therefore very strong – to send us into a very deep sleep.

We had no plans and had no idea how long we would stay there. Bamiyan was a very small place and we could easily walk around it in half an hour, so short of another expedition to the caves and the Buddhas there was not much else to do. Sikkendoah seemed to have a suggestion but we could not understand what he was trying to communicate.

The next morning, however, out and about, we met three other westerners who told us they wanted to go and see some lakes. They thought the name was something like Band-e Amir. This didn't mean anything to us but we suggested they come and talk to our charming host and see if we could communicate in some way -- and anyway, they were very keen to try his home-grown dope. When we mentioned the words sounding like 'Band-e Amir' Sikkendoah went into a frenzy of agreement and executed some excited jigs and we understood that this was what he had already tried to tell us about! He then took me by the hand and gestured the others to follow and we went off at a trot to meet a friend of his who had a small house and an ancient vehicle. It transpired that we could all hire the vehicle (for a ridiculously low price) and the friend would take us to these lakes. This sounded like rather a grand adventure and we were all happy to take the risk of setting off on an unknown expedition. It should always be remembered that we had no maps or guide books – we had no idea where we were going but simply relied on the foreigners' grapevine and a local's finger pointing somewhere. We always had to decide whether or not to trust the local and in this case we had had such good experiences with the Afghanis so far that we were ready to trust them and have faith that no difficulties would present themselves. So having paid the required fee we arranged to set off early the next morning.

More caring hosts we could never have. Early in the morning Sikkendoah woke us up and gave us tea and bread, his wife pressed a bag of food into our hands and they then led us off to the vehicle. I don't know what name to give to it! I suppose it was a cross between a kind of truck and a jeep fitted out with some wooden planks to make benches. Anyway, off we went. After four hours we were really beginning to wonder what we had let ourselves in for. The scenery was unremittingly dry and dusty desert with rocky outcrops. There was no road and the wheels threw up a fine dust so we were soon covered in white powder. All six of us looked like ghosts.

Then suddenly the vehicle stopped and the driver gesticulated to us to get off. But there was absolutely nothing there. As far as the eye could see there was just desert. I did start to feel a bit afraid – this man was not as charming as Sikkendoah – but he started walking off and beckoned to us to follow. It seemed almost as if we were blind because the sun was so bright there was no light or shade indicating ups or downs so we of necessity focussed on just a few feet ahead. It was a very disorientating feeling which became even frightening when the driver gave a warning shout and stopped dead. We fortunately stopped dead too otherwise we would have gone straight over a high cliff dropping sharply into a kind of valley hundreds of metres below us.

Teetering on the edge, we were stunned to see an incredible panorama. We were looking at a kind of cleft or crevice between two cliffs which was about half a mile wide and stretched for miles both left and right. Along the bottom of the crevice was a string of six lakes – like precious stones on a necklace – each coloured a different shade of blue ranging from light turquoise to the deepest Prussian blue, a shade almost inconceivable to find in nature. The lakes nestled against backgrounds sometimes of fine white sand, sometimes of coloured rock streaked with pink and orange and grey and pale yellow. And the rocks seemed to glisten as if they were studded with diamonds!

Except for a small shack near the biggest lake there was nothing and nobody there.

The driver got a bit impatient with our awed silence and walked off to the left indicating that we should follow. We then saw that there was a narrow path down which one could climb to get to the bottom. This was dangerous to an extreme but we had to go further, so down we struggled, clinging to any outcrop we could find to save ourselves from certain death if we fell.

The shack turned out to be a tea house so we restored shattered nerves with the welcome drink. We were closest to the prussian blue lake but we wandered off to the next one which was a deep turquoise. I was fascinated by the coloured striated rocks we were walking across and whatever mineral it was that they contained which caused them to sparkle like diamonds. The silence was so deep it seemed like we had gone deaf.

But after an hour or two the silence was broken by our driver who was calling us to return. Simon and Pieter and I looked at each other and we instantaneously agreed we could not leave this place so quickly. On the way back we had a hurried conference: could we somehow make the driver understand that we would pay him double if he would come back the next day to pick us up again? We had the bag of food and a bit of starvation would be tolerable – we could feast on the beauty – and for some reason Simon had brought his sleeping bag which unzipped so we could cover ourselves. We were so familiar with each other by now that that kind of close proximity was acceptable for one night. We didn't think we would sleep much anyway. It would be a risk to pay the driver up front right now as he might not come back and leave us there with unknown consequences but our new friends, who did want to go back to Bamiyan, said they would go and see Sikkendoah and tell him of our plan. It meant trust again but we decided to risk it.

When the driver saw the money and we pointed to watches and mimed twenty-four hours going by, he seemed to get the point and was amenable to the change in plan – so off he went with our new friends and we walked back to explore the other lakes.

We had no hallucinatory drugs with us, we just weren't into drugs, but it seemed as if we had imbibed a lot because that afternoon and night were surreal. It was so silent, the air was so clear, the water in the lakes was so pristine ... this was untouched, unsullied nature in total purity.

We walked for as long as we could then, after sitting down to eat our small meal, we were treated to a gentle sunset of pastel hues – there was no pollution and no clouds to create riotous colours – and watched in awe as the stars came out, first in a turquoise sky which slowly deepened to a midnight blue one. Finally a half-moon rose, lighting up the cliffs and reflecting itself in the very still water of the lake. It was cold and we were glad of the sleeping bag and dozed sporadically as the night wore on and turned into dawn. Nature then provided another drama of a rising sun and all the myriad of colours that accompanied it. The few pangs of hunger were easy to bear when faced with this splendour.

But existence decreed that we were not even to suffer that slight inconvenience because as the sun rose we heard a shout 'Sikkendoahhhhhhh' and there, at the top of the cliff, was our good friend yelling happily and waving his bright turquoise turban ebulliently. We just had to laugh at this apparition. He was such a force of nature! He somehow managed to scramble down the cliff and arrived, almost bouncing with enthusiasm, carrying another bag full of food for a breakfast picnic. Needless to say it all tasted divine.

We realised he had decided to come with the driver on the return journey to pick us up and when the man himself appeared we all companionably walked around one more lake before starting the journey back.

We spent another two days in Bamiyan, again visiting the Buddhas and absorbing as much of the meditative ambience around them as we could. We also found that there was a camp of the nomadic Kuchis just outside the village and tried to meet them and spend some time with them although they were not very friendly. I loved their embroidered clothes in bright colours, often with small circular pieces of metal sewn on as decoration. Many months later I was surprised to see very similar embroidery and styles amongst the rural Gujaratis when I visited remote places in that Indian province a few months later.

We had decided to spend time in Bamiyan rather than in Kabul because staying with Sikkendoah and his family was such a unique experience. From Bamiyan we planned to travel straight through to Delhi because time was moving on. Pieter had only a short time left to see some parts of India and I wanted to meet the American and see what might happen with him. Simon was relaxed about it all and planned to go with Pieter to Kulu Manali in the Himalayas. Even at that early time, it had become a well-known hippie haunt.

And so we regretfully left the unique Bamiyan and our very special hosts and journeyed by night bus back to Kabul where we caught another bus to Pakistan.

Bamiyan to Delhi – by truck, foot and train

irritating people and places, a hike in the heat, old and new friends

Chapter 6

I have no recollection of the trip from Kabul into Pakistan. This is quite strange as we would have had to have gone through one of the most famous mountain passes in the world: the Khyber Pass. I don't remember anything about it. I can only conclude that we travelled by night, managed to sleep and therefore missed it all.

We had to spend three nights in Pakistan but I am not even sure which city we stayed in − maybe Islamabad. This is a very good example of how one tends to blank something out when one doesn't like it. Because we hated Pakistan! It was horrible. Much worse than Iran. We were pestered and hassled unmercifully every minute, every metre, mostly by the male species − I cannot dignify them with the name 'men' − and beggars galore of both species and all ages.

We had no choice but to stay there because, bizarrely, although we didn't need a visa to enter the country, we had found out that we needed one to leave and had to buy it from some government office in the city. Unfortunately for us we arrived on a Friday afternoon and the office was closed until Monday morning so we had to wait until it opened. The whole city was filthy and the hotel we finally found, although better than others, broke every hygienic principle in the book. Usually the women in a country are nicer than the men but the female receptionist at this hotel was very rude and refused to let me share a room with the guys because she said I wasn't married to either one of them! So I had to have a small dirty room to myself with no lock on the door. I was outraged. Once everyone had gone to sleep I crept into Simon and Pieter's room with my sleeping bag as I gave myself no chances being alone in an unlocked room in such a horrible place.

My presence was like a red flag to a bull to the local male population so I stayed in this hotel for the whole weekend while Pieter and Simon ventured out on food-foraging expeditions. Monday finally came and we did an unheard of thing for us: we hired a taxi. Which shows how desperate we were to avoid the city. The taxi was a decrepit vehicle in dire condition and we were doubtful if it would even make it to the government office to obtain this hugely expensive exit visa. Getting the visa was fortunately quite quick – money talks–and when we came out of the office we found that the taxi driver had stayed in the hope of a further fare back to the city centre. We obliged him as we could not face any journey in a local city bus and we told him to take us straight to the bus station. It was with huge relief that we found we could get a decrepit vehicle which was leaving for the Indian border within an hour.

I don't remember anything of that journey beyond its massive discomfort. But after only a few hours we arrived at the border and were deposited in front of a row of tents which formed the Customs and Immigration offices. There was fortunately also a money-exchange kiosk. It was lucky that we had been warned about getting that exit visa because we met some western travellers who had not heard of the edict and had been ordered to return to Islamabad to get the exit visa before being allowed to leave.

The next hurdle to face was another situation we had been warned about. When we entered the Indian Customs and

Immigration tent, we were shepherded, one by one, into a small cubicle to face a slimy Indian woman who was rumoured to have psychic powers and who could, apparently, just by looking at you, decide whether or not you were smuggling drugs. There were reports that she was also known to plant drugs in your luggage or in a coat pocket or something to ostensibly discover and make you pay a huge fine. She was really creepy and sort of circled me closely, giving me strange vibes, before looking through my luggage. As I knew I didn't have anything I was not afraid but was still aware of the possibility of her planting stuff, so I watched her as closely as she watched me and tried to psyche her out by showing I was not afraid of her. She didn't like that at all but as she could not find anything incriminating she had to let me go and we finally all emerged at the exit, ruffled but unscathed.

We then found we had to walk to the Indian border along a path through a stretch of scrubby no-man's land about six miles long. We were hot, tired, thirsty, hungry and very bad-tempered by the time we reached the Indian border where the immigration process was thankfully only a formality and we could catch a local bus to the Amritsar train station a short trip away.

Arriving in Amritsar was a huge let-down. For the whole journey, India had been the golden goal, the mythical, magical place with so much promise of exciting unknown adventures both external and internal. Instead it wasn't much better than Pakistan. The Muslim element was still strong here which for me presented continual problems of being hassled the whole time. Despite wearing clothes as concealing as I could manage, and being escorted by two guys, men confronted me and attempted to grab me whenever they could. I call them 'men'; actually they were like irritating little boys, immature, ignoble, unpleasant. The women were nicer but their colourful saris were garish and almost theatrical in comparison to the subtle artistic hues of my Afghani friends. I suppose the truth was that I had fallen so much in love with Afghanistan and its people that India, in comparison, was lacking in every aspect.

For me personally there were other issues which for sure affected my perceptions. The bus deposited us at the Amritsar train station which was awash with the very familiar brilliant colours of bougainvillea and hibiscus flowers and other tropical shrubs with brightly coloured leaves. For Simon and Pieter this was an exotic scene but for me it brought back memories of South Africa where I was born and brought up and which I had left at the first opportunity. I had lived in Durban, a tropical city in which bougainvillea and hibiscus plants flourished in profusion, but my life there had not been great and I did not want to be suddenly reminded of it. There were many Indians in and around Durban because Indians had originally been brought over from India to work on the sugar cane fields and after five years had been freed and given the option of returning to India or staying. As life in South Africa was far more comfortable and promising than India, the majority chose to stay and indeed carved out prosperous lives for themselves here while retaining their Indian culture and heritage. But I had left South Africa to make a new life for myself and, after enjoying the chances to travel and meet many different kinds of people, I did not want to be reminded of my past everywhere I looked.

I was also worried about my health. Having been brought up in South Africa, I was very strong with a constitution of the proverbial ox and this had stood me in good stead while roaming the unfamiliar countries we had just passed through.

When my travelling companions had been beset with the travel bugs usual on this journey, I had been unaffected. But, prior to this trip, when I had been in the USA with Alex, I had been ill with a severe kidney infection which necessitated a stint in hospital and a course of heavy antibiotics. I was now aware of a pain in both my kidneys which meant that the infection had returned and I was now far away from any reliable medical facility.

This too presented a problem with Alex because one of the reasons he had not wanted me to accompany him to India was in case I got sick and he had to take care of me – a complication which he naturally didn't want to be concerned with. I totally understood his concern and did not want to be a burden on him and cause him this hassle, so I was really upset at the prospect of finally meeting him again only to present him with the problem he had gone to lengths to avoid.

I was tired and dirty after the whole Pakistan and border ordeal so when I saw a 'ladies' waiting room' on the train station I told the guys that I wanted to have a rest for a few hours until the next train left for Delhi.

In the USA I had studied about India alongside Alex while he was doing his research for his documentaries, and I remembered reading that the waiting rooms on the train stations in India were often elaborate affairs as they had been built by the British Raj to provide much needed respite on their journeys around the country. I struck gold with this one!

Beautifully furnished with carved wooden chairs and benches long enough to sleep on, it was clean and cool and quiet. Perfect for my nerves. As I put down my backpack an old Indian lady emerged from a small room, obviously her domain, and said 'Bath, madam?' Wow! This was even better than I had thought. It turned out that if I gave her a few rupees she would heat up some water and I could have a hot shower in the spotlessly clean bathroom she now showed me. We had fortunately changed some money at the border so I immediately agreed and after a hot shower, all clean and fresh again, my equanimity was considerably restored and I was in a more positive frame of mind – no doubt much to the relief of my companions – when we boarded the train to Delhi.

I filed this experience away in my brain for future reference and there would be many times in my travels around India that the ladies' waiting rooms on the train stations (and dak bungalows, also built by the British for a similar purpose) would provide a haven of cleanliness, coolness and quiet in this otherwise dirty, hot, continuously noisy and often irritating country.

Delhi was not too bad. There were some nice historical buildings in pink stone and some rather impressive Victorian or Georgian-style buildings, no doubt connected to the past British Raj regime. We had been told of a cheap hippie place to stay near the famous Connaught Place and managed to find our way there quite easily because many people here spoke English, so communication wasn't the guessing game it had hitherto been. Quite a relief. The accommodation was reasonable and after getting my sleeping place organised I told the guys I wanted to try to find the family whose address Alex had given me as a contact. It was easy to move around in Delhi because of the little three-wheeled vehicles called rickshaws, so I hailed one and showed the driver the address. He waggled his head in what I soon found was a 'yes', even though it looked like a 'no', and off we went into what looked like quite a well-to-do area with big houses and manicured lawns and loads of flowers everywhere. Even the rickshaw driver had a grasp of English because when I asked him to wait, he had no difficulty in understanding me. I went up to the door of a large, very well-kept house and knocked on the door. A kind of 'butler' allowed me inside and soon a very friendly woman came into the room. When she heard my request for information about Alex she got quite excited and told me that he had indeed contacted her and would arrive in Delhi in two days. She even had the arrival time of his train from Benares and suggested I could surprise him by meeting him. After pressing a cup of delicious chai (Indian-style tea made with a lot of milk and spices) and a plate of Indian sweets on me, I returned via my rickshaw to Connaught Place.

Even though I was alone I wasn't hassled much. Delhi is the seat of government in India so there were quite a number of non-hippie foreigners there: ambassadors, consuls, and business men etc. Foreigners weren't the rarity that they were in the other countries I had just passed through so I didn't feel I had to be as much on my guard.

I enjoyed being able to stroll around Connaught Place alone, in relative peace, and soon became fascinated with the shops and commodities on sale there. Connaught Place, often called Connaught Circle, had been conceived of as a market and business centre in the early 1900's and construction started around 1929. The plan, designed by a British architect, was for a circular plaza, modelled after the Royal Crescent in Bath, England, filled with shops, businesses, important government buildings and prestigious residences. It still fulfills those functions today, although there are now modern shopping malls and high-rise buildings. What I saw then was a much simpler and more gracious shopping centre and what fascinated me the most was the small shops selling locally created goods from all the many states of India. They were exotic and colourful and I was fascinated. There were also the 'khadi' shops selling hand-woven fabric and hand-made articles of clothing in cotton and silk. They were part of the so-called 'cottage industries' set up by Mahatma Gandhi to provide work and income for poor people and to preserve traditional ways of doing things.

My clothes were looking very scruffy by now and I was very happy to replenish my wardrobe with some 'kurtas' – long, loose-fitting shirts. I bought two cotton ones, one pink, one white, with embroidery stitched in white in the Chikan style and one pale blue one made of rough khadi silk. My two skirts were just holding up but I bought some cotton 'pyjama' pants for hanging out in. A few silver arm bracelets, an ankle bracelet and matching toe rings were added to the purchases, along with a new cloth shoulder bag and some chappals – Indian-style sandals. In a rather posh tearoom I then sat down to a really nice cup of tea with milk and sugar, all served from a silver tea set, and nibbled on the small cakes provided. Very British.

With this small taste of relative luxury, after the very rough conditions I had been living in for the past couple of months, I decided that my travel budget would stretch to a few days in a proper hotel where I could rest in comparative ease and hope that the kidney situation would improve. Also, if Alex was not averse to spending some time together he could join me if he wanted to. In all honesty I was not at all sure what our relationship would be as I knew I had changed a lot and he too would have undergone some interesting and very different experiences.

Having decided on this course of action, I returned to the hippie hang-out hoping to find Simon and Pieter to tell them of this plan, to see if they had any objections and also to find out if they had decided what the next step in our journey would be. Having found them, we adjourned to a little restaurant for some curry, and discussed plans. Pieter wanted to leave the next day to go to Kulu Manali in the Himalayas. Now a tourist holiday resort spoiled by unregulated tourism, Manali then provided an almost untouched experience of nature in the famous mountains, and it had become a bit of a hippie refuge, providing a peaceful respite from the rigors of the heavy travelling ordeals most people had been through. Pieter had only about ten days left before he would fly back to Germany from Delhi to start a new term at university. Simon was not constrained by this schedule but he thought he would go with Pieter as Manali was 'must see' on the hippie trial.

This meant that our ways must now part – which was a sobering thought. We had been through so much together and now we were quite suddenly faced with the end of our travels as we had so far known them. Uppermost in all our minds was: what if things with Alex did not work out? I would then be all alone in India. I was touched by their concern but I had already decided that if things did not work out with Alex and with the worry about my health, I would fly back to England. We decided to have a slap-up meal at one of the restaurants catering to western tastes and celebrate the great time we had had together and make a toast to future, equally extraordinary, adventures.

The next morning I saw them off on a train to the Himalayas and checked myself into a small comfortable hotel near Connaught Place. I definitely shed some tears because our whole journey had been a special and precious time – the personal friendships we had formed had been deep and heartful and the exotic places we had visited, the strangers we had met and the unexpected events we had experienced had incredibly enriched our lives.

It was not an easy sleep I had that night and waiting on the station platform for Alex's train to arrive, I was experiencing both misgivings and trepidation at what now might be in store. To make matters worse, the pain in my kidneys had increased and I could feel that I was beginning to run a slight fever.

Alex was very much his charming self and had matured and taken on a very decisive and business-like manner but it was soon apparent that on a personal level, from both sides, we were friends but no more. We had both changed and gone in different directions. He said, however, that he had a bit of business to do in Delhi and would be there for a few days during which time we could meet and share stories of our travels. This was all good except that the next morning my fever was worse and when I met him in the morning I confessed that I was not up to doing anything and in fact needed help.

I could see that he was exasperated with having to deal with this situation but immediately took me to see an Indian doctor in a building near the woman who had been our 'go-between'. Alex explained that when he had lived in India a few years before, this was the doctor he and his fellow students had to been referred to. Doctor Khan was in fact the doctor used by foreign officials from embassies and foreign business people and had a good reputation. It seemed that an appointment was available within an hour and Alex left me there to do some business while I waited in the spotlessly clean waiting-room. Dr Khan was great. After giving me a thorough examination he told me he wanted to treat my condition not by giving antibiotics, but by using remedies developed by the Indian Ayurvedic system of medicine. He said that kidney complaints were common in India as it was easy to get dehydrated in such a hot climate, and many traditional treatments had been developed. He then frightened me horribly, however, by saying he wanted me to go into hospital as it was important to have an internal examination to make sure there was no physical cause for the ongoing infections. He wanted me in hospital immediately – to be treated and to prepare for the examination which would take place early the next morning.

Well, it seemed that that was the end of my rendezvous with Alex so rather frustrated I got into a rickshaw, went back to my hotel, told them I would be away for two nights but to keep my room anyway – I paid for it in advance – left a note for Alex telling him what had transpired and set off for this hospital. I was rather dreading what I might find, having heard some nightmare stories of Indian hospitals, but this was a nice place, run by nuns, very clean and organised. I was alone in a room with three beds. By now I was feeling pretty bad and after a nurse had come and given me my first dose of bright red medicine, I fell asleep.

Dr Khan arrived in the evening after I had been given a very good supper and told me I would need to have an anesthetic for the internal examination in the morning and should spend the following day and night in the hospital to recover. This was not welcome news but I could do nothing else except surrender to the situation and trust in his expertise. After two more doses of his medicine I was already feeling a bit better so that gave me a bit of confidence.

But Alex didn't come to visit so I resigned myself to facing this ordeal alone.

At the crack of dawn the next morning I was woken up and wheeled into an operating room where a mask was placed over my nose and I knew no more. When I finally regained consciousness a few hours later I was back in my room – with a gorgeous-looking western man sitting by my bedside holding my hand! Bewildered, I closed my eyes and opened them again only to find that the person was still there and softly saying my name. My first thought was: Am I hallucinating? What had they given me on that operating table? But as my eyes focussed I saw that this was no apparition but a real person and that he was smiling sympathetically at me, obviously understanding my confusion. He told me his name was John and then called a nurse to say that I was now conscious.

He disappeared while I was given another dose of medicine and some toast and a banana and had a bit of a wash and a brush-up. When he later returned I was feeling a great deal better and curious as to who this very good-looking stranger was. He told me that he had been in India for nearly a year studying music – sitar and flute – in Benares, but had been up to Kulu Manali for a holiday where he had contracted the dreaded Hepatitis B – the bane of westerners in India. When he was strong enough to move he had come down to Delhi and checked himself into this hospital for treatment and good food.

He had noticed my arrival and had found it strange that I should be alone so took it upon himself to be a friend. I was very touched by his kindness; and the fact that he was so good-looking was, of course, an added bonus. We chatted most of the day and I was really feeling better by the time Dr Khan arrived in the evening. He told me that the internal examination had revealed no problems and that, as long as I continued to take the medicine for the required time and rested for a few more days, I would be fit and strong again. He added that I could leave the hospital the next morning.

I had told John about Alex and my current travelling dilemma and he said that if I wanted to, I could come and visit him in Benares — to which he would return in a few days — and maybe join up with some people there. He said there were quite a few westerners there: the usual hippies but also some people studying music, art, Hindi or Sanskrit at Benares Hindu University. This was actually the university where Alex had studied. Before I left he told me that if I decided to come to Benares I should go to Assi Ghat, find the chai wallah (a man who serves chai or tea) there and ask him to take me to John's house.

John already seemed like a good friend but I was rather hurt that Alex hadn't contacted me so I wanted to return to my hotel and find out what had happened. In my heart of hearts I knew, however, that this inconvenient illness had scuppered any chance of any kind of connection with him and I should be prepared for the consequences. When I got back to the hotel, there was a letter from him saying that he had had to leave for the next lot of filming and that he was sorry but there could be no further meetings with him. I totally understood but felt a bit bereft and also a bit scared at having to make a decision about what I would do next: go to Benares or back to England? For the moment, though, it was important to get my health firmly back on track so I decided to buy a book in one of the English bookshops in Connaught Place and rest in my hotel room for another two days. It was a good book and a good rest and the next day I ventured out for some food, feeling much restored, with a decision made to leave any life-changing choices for at least one more day.

And then fate fortuitously intervened to lend a hand! On my way to my now favourite little restaurant I heard my name being called and turned to see Hans and Dietrich, my German friends who I had last seen in Iran, waving frantically and running towards me. With hugs all round we quickly sat down for some tea and babbled simultaneously as we tried to catch up with all our adventures. They had had an amazing time exploring untravelled far-away areas in northern regions of Afghanistan, Pakistan and India (Giovanni had decided to spend more time in the Himalayas) and were now on their way to Benares via a southern route to see the Taj Mahal and the Khajuraho temples. From Benares they would take a train back to Delhi and fly home to Germany. I was welcome to travel with them if I wanted to.

How generous existence was to arrange things so perfectly! It would be terrible to leave India without seeing the Taj Mahal, so travelling with these good friends I could visit this famous monument and also meet up with John in Benares. I would leave it to existence to then decide where else my path should lead to.

Delhi to Benares – by train and bus

monuments of splendour, flitting fireflies, religious dramas,
the holy city

Chapter 7

The railway system in India was possibly the greatest achievement of the British Raj. Apart from the fact that the engines and carriages were ancient − museum specimens, I should think − and that the actual train schedule bore no resemblance to the published one, trains running from two to ten hours late; and that one had to stand in a mile-long queue to get a ticket (I think right here I could write a short book on travelling on Indian trains in the early 1970's) … one actually could manage, very cheaply, to get from A to B. Eventually.

And so Hans, Dietrich and I decided to go south to see the Taj Mahal in Agra, Uttar Pradesh, by train.

Joining the long queue at the crack of dawn we eventually managed to get tickets and the train left only an hour and a half late. Even in an Indian train, the journey took only a few hours so we arrived mid-afternoon, found a small, relatively clean hotel and got ready to visit this magnificent monument in the evening because it was close to full moon and one of course HAS to see the Taj Mahal on a full moon night.

No photograph, no gushing description, can ever convey the magical, ethereal splendour of this edifice. I am not going to try. Suffice it is to say that it truly deserves every accolade thrown at it, and then more, and I count myself immensely fortunate that my first glimpse of this exquisite tomb -- built by Shah Jahan for his beloved wife Mumtaz Mahal -- was by moonlight with almost no other people around. The place was silent except for the sound of the river and we tip-toed around without voicing even a hushed whisper as we absorbed enough beauty to last a lifetime.

The impact was not only visual. The place had such a quality of meditation that one's body became almost transparent as one melted into the delicately carved white marble tracery and disappeared into an enchanted state cast by this otherworldly tribute to a loved one.

We decided on a second visit the next morning to see the daylight face of the building. While not as atmospheric as the moonlit view, we were able to savour many more precious aspects of one of the greatest artistic and architectural feats of the world.

Then, in the afternoon, after a short siesta dreaming white marble fantasies, we took a taxi to a deserted city about forty kilometres away from Agra called Fatehpur Sikri. This city was built in pink sandstone by the Emperor Akbar in the sixteenth century as his capital city. But after ten years he left to fight invading Afghan armies and made a new capital in Lahore, never to return to his architectural wonder which was sadly very soon deserted because of the lack of an adequate water supply. In a very different way we were deeply impressed by the intricately carved Mughal temples, mosques, arched colonnades and the magnificent entrance gate. At the end of the rocky plateau on which the centre of the city was built, was a drop of about three hundred feet at the bottom of which was a deep pool. From a platform at the top, servants used to dive into the pool for the entertainment of the court.

We were not royalty but as we were the only people there we felt like the place belonged to us and we enjoyed the feeling of wandering at will, imagining ourselves as wealthy royal members of Akbar's court.

I feel privileged indeed to have visited these breathtakingly beautiful marvels at this time, long before the inroads of mass tourism robbed one of the possibility of savouring these places in silence and solitariness.

Back in Agra we wandered around the small town looking at the local craftsmen who carved the typical 'kari' artefacts such as small boxes, decorative mirrors etc. Kari is a decorative art formed by inlaying semi-precious or precious stones into a design carved into a marble base. There are many examples of this work in the Taj Mahal and it is still today a thriving 'cottage industry' in the streets of Agra.

As the daylight faded I saw, to my excitement, my first elephant walking down the road. There must have been a celebration of sorts, perhaps a marriage, as the elephant wore a garb of brightly-coloured embroidered cloth and musicians, discordantly playing a loud trumpet-type of instrument, preceded it while men pranced around in an uncoordinated dance.

Then, sated with all the wonders we had seen in the past twenty-four hours, we slept deeply and woke early to catch a bus to our next destination: the temples of Khajuraho.

Now there are rail connections to the town of Khajuraho, and even an airport, because these temples have become one of the must-see tourist sights in India. Then there was only a pot-holed dirt road over which our dilapidated, rattling, unsprung bus made its way at a snail's pace, stopping every few metres it seemed, to pick up or deposit a passenger. We had no idea where we would stay when we got to the small village but we were met at the bus stop by a determined Indian lady who insisted we stay at her guest house. As it was the only place to stay we had no choice, but anyway it was adequate enough: basic concrete floors and walls, iron beds, but clean with a washing area. A far cry from the five-star honeymoon hotels prolific in the area today.

There appeared to be no place to eat, but our host was happy to offer a home-cooked meal for a fee so we sat on her kitchen floor and, after firmly limiting the amount of curry powder and chillies she wanted to use, we ate a very reasonable meal off washed banana leaves.

The next morning we found a chai shop and had some suji – a kind of porridge made from coarsely ground wheat – and, watched by curious locals, wandered off to the deserted temples. No attempt had been made to take care of the buildings; the whole area was untidy and unkempt with weeds growing everywhere. We actually had to brush the undergrowth aside in order to walk along the paths of broken stone to the buildings. The carved erotic statues covering every inch of the surface of the temples have now been photographed and displayed the world over in books and on the internet, but we had not seen even one image so I must confess we were quite shocked at such graphic scenes of sexuality. We had heard a bit about something called tantra in India but the significance of what I was seeing totally escaped me. I simply could not understand the connection of such subject matter with religion. After the exquisite beauty of the Taj Mahal, at which we had gazed in wonder just two days before, this display seemed crass and crude and after an hour we lost interest and went back to our little guest house for an afternoon nap.

Having swallowed most of my prescribed red medicine, my kidney complaint had now pretty much disappeared but Hans was not feeling well at all so, to give him a chance to rest, we decided to stay one more night before moving on to Benares by bus and train, a potentially tough journey as we were very much off the beaten track. The two guys had now only a few days left in India before flying home.

When she heard of our plans, our landlady, who spoke a few words of English, got quite excited and, pointing in another direction, said 'Ram Leela! Ram Leela!' The guys looked at me blankly but a bell was ringing in my brain and I remembered that Alex had mentioned that he was busy filming some festivals in various localities. This month was the month of the Ram Leela Festival that takes place throughout northern India in the autumn. Towns and villages put on traditional performances based on the Hindu religious epic, the Ramayana, which depicts the life of Lord Ram and ends in a long battle between him and the demon king, Ravana. Ram, of course, triumphs.

Hans decided that he needed to rest, so that evening Dietrich and I set off in the direction of the pointing finger and, to our surprise, the short road we followed presented a spectacle which far surpassed world-famous erotic temples and traditional epic dramas. The sun had just set, leaving a softly colourful silent twilight, and, stretching before us, we saw a road flanked on either side with 'lollipop' trees – trees with straight trunks and foliage making a perfectly round shape – which formed almost a tunnel through which we had to pass.

Each tree was covered with a mass of flitting fireflies – like winking Christmas tree fairy lights or thousands and thousands of dancing Tinkerbells. As we entered the 'tunnel' it really felt like we were entering a glittering enchanted fairyland – totally unreal and magical.

Bemused by this mesmerising display, it was a little difficult to continue our journey towards the drama event but we pulled ourselves together, returned to reality and followed a now growing noise of shouts and laughter. It was a joyful scene that met our eyes. In the centre of a little village, a stage had been erected and an energetic performance was being enacted. Light was provided by burning flares which added to the exotic nature of the drama and the audience of enrapt villagers was totally caught up with what was going on onstage. They didn't even notice us as we slipped into spaces at the back. What was strange was that the audience was neatly and firmly divided into two by some ropes: the men sat together on the left and the women sat together on the right. We did likewise. I was amazed at how good the actors were and even though I couldn't understand a word, I was quickly swept up in the local enthusiasm and was soon laughing and yelling along with everybody else.

After an hour or so there appeared to be no imminent end to the performance and we eventually decided to leave as we had an early start the next morning. Sadly the fireflies must have gone to sleep for the night because our fairyland path was in darkness. Perhaps they only came out at twilight.

The next morning Hans was feeling a little better so we decided to push on as we were not at all sure of bus and train connections to the east of Khajuraho. We were really going into the untravelled interior of the continent. Fortunately or unfortunately, wherever we went, we were surrounded by people fascinated by such strange beings. This could be a pain but it proved often to be an asset because invariably there was one person who spoke some English – maybe a village teacher or a returned student – and they were always eager to demonstrate their language skills and badger us with questions. We, in turn, could question them and get required travel information. So we learnt that we could get a bus to a place called Satna where we could pick up a train coming up the more eastern side of India from Nagpur, through Jabalpur, ending up in Benares.

It was a relatively short distance but it took a long time because the local bus was the usual decrepit one taking its time to wander around various villages. We had to wait a long time for the next train and when it finally did appear it turned out to be one of those painfully slow ones that stopped for hours at every small station. It was also jam-packed with people and there was no possibility of a seat so we had to sit on the floor by the door. A primitive toilet was fortunately available close by because poor Hans was still ill and alternated his time between sitting on the toilet and stretched out as best he could on the limited dirty floor space available. We felt so sorry for him.

An additional problem was lack of something to drink because dehydration is a real danger when someone has bad diarrhoea. Safe bottled water was unheard of at that time so we had to make do with coca colas which, being made by an American company, had proved to be relatively safe to drink but not great for one's stomach. Fortunately chai vendors were a feature of every Indian train station and, because the water had been boiled, we usually drunk it. Little disposable clay pots were always a preference as they were discarded after use − but glasses were suspect as the chai wallah would quickly rinse them in filthy cold water after serving one customer and then refill them for the next one! The build-up of so many germs was a nightmarish thought.

It was a very, very long journey but finally, as dawn was breaking, we slowly crossed the Ganges on a long bridge and arrived at an already busy Benares train station, slightly reeling from the unexpected splendour of the exotic, early morning scene we had just witnessed.

Benares
a fascinating, yet often disturbing, city

Chapter 8

As the train had approached Benares and crossed a bridge over the Ganges, we had been presented with a panoramic view of the oldest part of the ancient city, the sky and the river. The sky was ablaze with orange, pink and gold from the rising sun; the river was ablaze with the same colours reflected in its broad expanse which flowed slowly beneath us. Along the banks was a disordered profusion of temples all bathed in rosy hues, and down rows of steps flocked crowds of worshippers seeking a spiritual dip in the holy water to start off the day. Brightly coloured flower petals strewn on the surface of the water mingled with the brightly coloured saris of the women and the ochre robes of the many sadhus intent on their morning worship.

This finally was the India we had travelled so far to see! Benares, the spiritual capital of India and its oldest city, is venerated by Hindus, Buddhists and Jains alike – and for the first time we caught a glimpse of the spiritual heritage of these great religions which stretches back for thousands of years.

But before we had time to assimilate the magical wonder of what we were seeing, we were plunged into the noise and chaos of the train station and the magic disappeared as we were forced to come down to earth to grapple with the reality of everyday India.

At every station there was a crowd of people hassling us to choose the hotel they represented. Usually we would shop around but this morning we were very tired from our pretty tough journey so we followed the first 'agent' who managed to collar us and we ended up at quite a nice little hotel near the river. At that point we were willing to pay a few extra rupees for some comfort. But, it seemed, we were too early and the previous night's guests had not left yet, so no room was available. However, the rather cheery receptionist promised that one would be ready in an hour and suggested that in the meantime we could leave our luggage with him and go for an early morning row on the river. He said that this was the best way to see Benares in the early morning. After insisting on a receipt for the luggage we followed the pointing finger again and found ourselves at the water's edge. A small rowing boat quickly materialised, a charge decided on (to avoid disputes it was always important to decide on a charge before, rather than after, any event) and we were rowed out into the river and upstream. Although those early morning colours had now faded we were able to see, in more fascinating detail, the buildings, people and activities along the river bank.

Even more people had arrived to do their river ablutions and it was amazing watching the variety of people there. As well as the colourful spectacle we also became aware of all kinds of music being played, and there was one sound which I associate to this day with early mornings in Benares -- but more about that later.

Not far from the moorings of our little boat was a 'burning ghat' and already chanting could be heard, rising smoke could be seen and a faintly sickening smell spread across the water. We remembered that Benares, as the most spiritual place in India, was an important place to die. If someone died here he was guaranteed to escape the wheel of birth and death and go straight to heaven, rather than having to return in another body to work on his accrued karmas. Anybody who could afford it came to Benares to die and be burnt at one of the burning ghats, have his ashes scattered over the holy Ganges and so be delivered to heaven. Death was consequently big business in this city.

The rather grim reality of all this was soon to be brought home to us. A few minutes later, amidst the usual debris floating down the river, we saw what appeared to be a bundle of rags floating on the surface of the water and receiving the attentions of a big black crow. The bundle finally bobbed against the side of the boat, a horrible smell arose and we saw to our horror that the bundle was a bloated dead body. I remembered from my India studies that people who were too poor to afford the wood and ceremonies of a burning ghat, just threw the dead bodies of their relatives into the water believing that such a burial would be as effective at freeing the person from his karmas as being burnt. Witnessing this firsthand in one's first few hours in the city was, however, a very gruesome experience.

This incident perhaps typifies the bewildering mass of contradictions that Benares presented: it was a city of stunningly magnificent vistas, great and small – a photographer's paradise – and a city of extreme poverty, squalor and misery such as I have never seen anywhere else, before or since. At that time the Ganges Basin was the most heavily populated area in the world and for many, life was one long suffering effort to survive.

With rather dampened spirits we returned to our small hotel to find a room with three beds mercifully clean and ready and we were able to have showers, welcome cups of hot chai and a few hours of sleep.

Waking in the mid-afternoon, we found we were actually quite refreshed and revitalised by the energy of the city. Hans, in particular, was very much better (was it due to the famed healing properties of the Mother Ganges?) so we set out to explore the city because time for the guys was running out. They needed to return to Delhi the following evening in order to catch their plane back to Germany. To that end our first stop was the train station as berths on an overnight train were paramount. Because of the Ram Leela festivities, berths were very much at a premium and the guys were forced into buying first class tickets, something none of us had ever done before! They fortunately had almost enough money and I contributed a top-up so that they could travel in comfort.

Benares has to be one of the most fascinating cities in the world. I use the present tense here because, as well as my conclusion then, it is also the opinion of friends who have visited the city recently. In the old city centre life is abundant in such profusion, with so many facets, that your senses are almost overwhelmed as you struggle through the milling crowds down tiny narrow streets sporting tiny shops on either side selling the most exotic of goods. Glorious colour, exotic fragrances – both of incense and of food – and endless music mingle in one surreal flow until it is almost too much to absorb.

After a few hours, it definitely was too much and we decided to wind our way back to the quieter area of our hotel – hoping that we could indeed find the way! Fortunately we soon realised we only had to go downstream along the river and, after circumventing the burning ghat with dogs gnawing on human bones, we found our hotel with relief and settled down for an early night and a very long, sound sleep.

The next morning Hans and Dietrich wanted to see an old

observatory built a few hundred years before. Having no guide books it took some time to find our way there although it actually wasn't too far from the hotel. We also had no explanation for what we were looking at but still it was rather impressive and a haven of peace and quiet in the noisy overcrowded city. The observatory was now in ruins but we were all intrigued by what were obviously astronomical instruments built from stone – looking a bit like sundials and sextants – and the floor looked like a decorated compass complete with markings of what appeared to be star constellations. This was a sight I had not expected to see in this holy city but it was yet one more part of the rich tapestry and mystery of the place.

We had planned a farewell lunch together after which I would leave for Assi Ghat upstream and try to find John while Hans and Dietrich would prepare for their final journey home. I confess that, as well as feeling sad at saying goodbye to such good friends and travelling companions, I was quite nervous at being on my own once more. I had no idea if I would even be able to find John, who was, after all, a complete stranger, but I told myself that things had somehow always worked out before so there was no reason for this situation to be any different. I reassured myself that if they didn't work out I could always get on a plane and go back to England. Nothing to be afraid of!

* * *

Hans and Dietrich came with me to find a bicycle rickshaw to take me to Assi Ghat and then it was really time to say goodbye. My feelings were quite confused as I waved to them from the rickshaw and then settled down to face the next adventure. My driver spoke no English but eventually he started to say 'Assi Ghat' and looked enquiringly at me for further instructions. It was a big place and a long road and I had no other information about where I was going, but when I said 'chai wallah' he seemed to be satisfied and soon stopped at one of the small shops that then abounded in India, selling milk and curd (yogurt) and sweet Indian chai.

The chai wallah looked at me without surprise so I assumed that there were some western people around and when I said 'John' he nodded his head and gestured to me to sit down. 'So far, so good', I thought, and had a very good cup of chai while I awaited further developments. I guess that in all the conversations that followed someone must have been summoned to give him a break and finally another man arrived to take over chai duties and the chai wallah beckoned me to follow him. We walked through a maze of tiny narrow streets, eventually ending up in a small two-storied building with a central courtyard. To the right of the entrance was a very small room with a door only of bars so I could see inside. The chai wallah pointed to the room and said 'John' and then departed, duty done! As a sitar was on prominent display in this little room I thought that this probably was John's abode but as there was nobody around, there was no-one to ask, so I obviously just had to sit and wait.

It was a long wait but eventually, after a few hours, John did show up. He was quite startled to see me and I felt rather worried that my arrival would cause him some inconvenience, but he was soon very welcoming and took me down to the river's edge, not far away, to chat and catch up on events since we last met in the Delhi hospital – actually not so long ago but I had travelled a lot since then so it seemed much longer. He said that he had almost fully recovered from the hepatitis, thanks to that hospital and the same Dr Khan, and had returned to Benares two days before and was getting back into his life here.

We then returned to the house and found that there was more activity. There was an Australian guy and his girlfriend who, despite looking very hippyish, were both studying Sanskrit at Benares Hindu University, not too far away. They had assumed Indian names – Kavi and Kavida – because they were followers of the Beatles' guru, Maharishi Mahesh Yogi. It turned out that someone else living in the little compound was away for a few days and I could rent his room while I looked around for a more permanent place. Rooms, it seemed, were quite easy to rent because the locals were glad of some extra income. There was a communal kitchen here so we cooked a meal of rice, dhal, vegetables and chapattis and had a very pleasant quiet evening just chatting about our various lives. I learnt that there was a small group of about ten westerners of different nationalities in the area, mostly studying Sanskrit or music.

Kavi was also able to answer a very urgent question I had: was it possible to have money transferred here from England? As the answer was yes, I could relax as I was beginning to get a bit worried about my finances.

The next morning, after a good sleep in the comfortable little room, I went with John to visit the chai wallah. He was apparently the local networker and letting agency. He also served the best curd I have ever tasted and I was soon a confirmed curd addict, as indeed were most of the other westerners around. We congregated at his shop for morning chai and curd and sweets from a sweet shop next door. The sweets quickly became another addiction. John spoke a bit of Hindi and it seemed that a search for a room for me would be

Initiated immediately. Two days later, in fact, a man came to our compound to say he had a place to rent. We all followed him and were quite surprised at the very beautiful room that he showed us.

It was huge, at least twenty by thirty feet, with three windows looking out over the Ganges. Attached was a small washroom and toilet (which emptied into a rather obvious sewer) and a little kitchen. The place was bare except for an old antique wooden bed.

A heated bargaining session began but as Kavi and Kavida both spoke Hindi I let them speak on my behalf. They were also experts in this kind of thing. The place was apparently comparatively expensive because it was part of an old Raja's palace and, though run down by our standards, it was a 'prestigious address'! I say 'comparatively expensive' because the final cost was a hundred rupees a month with four extra rupees for electricity. In those days there were about ten rupees to a British pound (depending on how hard you could bargain in the local black market) so that meant the rent was about £10. Having found that I could get money sent to the local Bank of India, I decided that this rent was affordable – it would be nice to settle and have my own space alone for a while – so the deal was struck, the rent was paid (lots of witnesses in case of future disputes) and I was given some rusty keys for an ancient padlock.

Setting up a little home took minimal effort because there were lots of small shops in the area selling basic household goods. Essential was a means to boil water to make tea so I bought a little paraffin stove, a container of paraffin, cooking pots and some cups and spoons. Milk I could get from the chai wallah, and I didn't want to do any more cooking than that because eating in small restaurants was cheap and easy and as long as everything was well cooked it was reasonably safe. There was also a very good Chinese restaurant nearer the Benares Hindu University and we incongruously ate Chinese spring rolls at every opportunity.

Benares was (still is) a city famed for its crafts. On the one hand there was the rather 'primitive' method of patterning cloth by using wood blocks carved into various patterns, pressed into different coloured dyes and then printed onto the fabric. In this way very attractive traditional designs on six-metre lengths of cotton for saris or larger pieces of cloth for bedcovers were made. I could not resist buying one of these to make my new room cosier.

On the other hand there was the very sophisticated craft of weaving exotically coloured lengths of silk with pure gold thread into intricate designs, making the very costly silk saris for which Benares was famous. People came from all over India to buy these saris for lavish wedding ceremonies.

It was quite an amazing experience to be wandering down a small path between scruffy run-down buildings, amidst squalor and extreme poverty, and to suddenly come upon a six-metre length of bright turquoise or vibrant orange silk being covered in intricate gold embroidery by a shoddily-clad man or woman.

But before savouring all the strange sights the most important task was to go to the Bank of India and arrange for money to be sent to me. I was dreading the task. When posting a letter took a day of hard work, what would be involved in getting money here?! Fortunately, because of various westerners studying at the University, the bank did actually have the necessary processes set up and it took only a few hours to thread my way through the maze of Indian bureaucracy. I finally got names, numbers and addresses and all I had to do then was to telegram a friend in England and ask her to send the money. This took another two or three hours because I also wanted her to wire me back to say that she had got my message. Then all I could do was wait – first for her reply and then for the money to arrive, which according to the bank, would take at least a month.

Within three days I got a return telegram from my friend to say that she had managed, also after about two hours in her bank, to get the money transferred. I heaved a huge sigh of relief, relaxed and set about exploring this ancient city in depth.

My most favourite thing by far was to sit by the ghats (stone steps leading down to the river) as the sun rose and watch the extraordinary scenes, the myriad assortment of people – and monkeys – and listen to the sound of the shenais as they sounded from temples around the city to herald the early morning worship. To this day the sound of the shenai evokes those early mornings by the Ganges for me.

A shenai is a wind instrument popular in northern India. It is made of wood with a metal 'trumpet-like' flare at the end and is played during religious ceremonies and special occasions like marriages. It was originally a kind of folk instrument but the famous Indian musician, Ustad Bismillah Khan, experimented and promoted its use in classical Indian music so it became more widely known.

Bismillah Khan's family home was in Benares and he was in residence while I was there so we were very fortunate to be able to attend his concerts which took place just in the streets. After about 10pm a platform would be dragged out into the middle of the street, some grass mats were spread on the ground, a few naked light bulbs would be hung perilously suspended from window ledges, and we would all gather round until about midnight when the Khan family would come out to play almost until dawn. Bismillah Khan's son was apparently an up and coming prodigy on the tabla drums. It was a surreal setting and again I was aware of the deep down mystery of the ancient culture of India. This was heightened when, after about the third concert we attended, Ustad, the master, invited us into his home to sit and have chai. It was an experience of something very deep and spiritual. I was fortunate indeed to have met him and experienced his music in such an informal but very real 'grass-roots' way.

One other musical event sticks in my mind. Amongst our group there was another American who was studying a little-known instrument, a veena. Whereas a sitar has one small resonating gourd to form the drum and is played with the drum resting on the left foot crossed under the right knee, the veena has two very large gourds and is played with the instrument placed almost horizontally in front of the performer. Only a few teachers existed then (fewer now) but so great was the American's love for the instrument that he would go once a week to Delhi (a ten hour train journey each way) for a lesson. I was very impressed and was to remember this meeting a few months later.

After a few days of not going anywhere I started to get a bit restless and decided to visit Sarnath, which was the deer park where Buddha gave his first discourse on the Dharma. It was about twelve kilometres from Benares and John said that I just had to catch the bus marked 'Sarnath'. He omitted to mention that it would be written in Hindi so I couldn't read the sign and nobody around seemed to be able to point me in the right direction. I decided then that it was time to learn some Hindi. Kavida took me to an old pundit, a teacher, who had been teaching at Benares Hindu University but had now retired. He was such a lovely old man and spoke good English so I enrolled for a course of lessons immediately. I had an hour long lesson every day and really enjoyed not only learning the language, but learning so much more about Indian ways, thoughts and history. The pundit had worked closely with Annie Besant, president of the Theosophical Society, when she created the Central Hindu College in Benares. Working with the Indian Government she then established the Benares Hindu University and my pundit was one of the first teachers of Sanskrit and Hindi at this new university.

Simple basic Hindi is a comparatively easy language to learn once the fifty-two characters have been mastered and I proudly took myself off to Sarnath two weeks later having very easily read the sign on the bus.

Given the direction my life took only a few months later, I am surprised, when I look back, that the whole spiritual ambience of Benares didn't touch me more. Kavida had tried to teach me transcendental meditation but I saw no point in sitting with my eyes closed, chanting a strange sound by the side of the river when, with eyes open, I could feast them on the glorious early morning river scenes. Beauty was always my thing.

Or, in hindsight, was it that the Zen philosophies of countries further east lay dormant inside me waiting to be lit by a different spark?

It was getting cold and John told me he would soon follow the hippie trail to Goa. Over the last few years it had become something of a tradition for hippies to spend Christmas in Goa, a small state on the west coast of India, south of Bombay, colonised by the Portuguese in the sixteenth century. Now Goa has changed almost beyond recognition and is filled with luxury resorts and all the ugly trappings of run-away mass tourism and package tours; at that time it was an untouched, unspoiled tropical paradise.

I could not move because I had to wait for my money to arrive but when one of the French music students said he would like to go to Nepal for a week and invited me to come along, I jumped at the chance. Hopefully the money would have arrived on my return and I could join John in Goa later. Some sun and sea and cleanliness sounded very attractive.

Much as I was enchanted with Benares, the smell and filth from the lack of toilets, open, often blocked and overflowing, sewers and hundreds of ownerless cows dropping cow pats everywhere augmented by dog doo deposited by another few thousand stray dogs, was beginning to get on my nerves. The suffering and misery of humans and animals, caused by the grinding poverty, was getting to me, as was the unwanted attentions of the many unemployed men around. Despite the tantric tradition, repressed sexual hang-ups lay just beneath the surface and all too often, while enjoying my explorations of the many facets of the city, I was subjected to a grinning guy whipping out his willy in front of me and ostentatiously peeing in the road or against a wall, all the time slyly watching to see my reaction. A legitimate form of flashing, I suppose!

It was time to move on.

The Frenchman wanted to fly into Kathmandu by plane as the view was said to be stunning – but my finances would not stretch that far. Kavi, however, offered to lend me the money for the ticket as he knew that my top-up funds would arrive sooner – or later – so I was guaranteed to return to Benares! Plans were made. I did not want to stay in Benares when I came back so I gave away the few bits and pieces I had acquired and once more packed the old backpack. We all went to the train station together to say goodbye to John who would be travelling west to Delhi. Then the Frenchman and I exchanged farewells with Kavi and Kavida as we set off east to catch a plane in the nearby city of Patna which even in those days had a small airport.

Benares to Kathmandu to Delhi
– by plane, bus and train
aerial views of the Himalayas, an infected big toe,
a journey of fear, sun rising over Everest

Chapter 9

The plane waiting on the runway in Patna looked alarmingly small. I think it only seated about ten people. It was too late to turn back now, however, so the Frenchman and I climbed in and fastened our seat belts for the relatively short flight to Nepal – about two hours.

The flat Ganges basin gave no hint of the mountains ahead of us but as we rose higher, the first range of mountains appeared and then white capped mountain tops arose in the far distance – frustratingly only partially seen out of the small windows. But then the captain invited us into the cockpit and suddenly we were viewing an awesome panoramic one-hundred-and-eighty degree sweep of the Himalayas on the far side of a wide valley. It was very definitely stunning! The pilot pointed out Mt Everest to us although I am not sure I could distinguish it from all the other mountain tops. The mind, however, could play nice games with the concept of seeing the most famous mountain in the world.

All too soon we were descending into the valley and landing just outside Kathmandu. The Frenchman had the address of a small hotel/guesthouse which we found quite easily but which was pretty dire. The rooms were dark, damp, dirty and very cold and I really didn't want to stay there. There was, however, some kind of local festival going on and the few places of accommodation were all full (and probably not much better) so we had to put up with it. That actually set the tone for my time in Nepal because I can't say that I liked much of what I saw. Throw in one of the most frightening experiences in my life and I was glad to leave a week later.

There were two good things.... I was sharing a room with an Australian girl called Liz and she was great: down-to-earth, funny and very vibrant and alive. Meeting her was the best part of the trip. There were very few women travelling alone at that time, for obvious reasons, so when we did meet up it was a very happy novelty. I wished I could have travelled further with Liz, it would have been good fun, but she was leaving to go back home after her visit to Nepal. The other good thing, which Liz introduced me to, was carrot halva. This was a sweet made by boiling milk, grated carrots and sugar together until they made almost a solid mass. Into this kind of fudge sludge, copious amounts of pistachio nuts were stirred and the confection was left to solidify. It was then cut into strips for you to eat. And it was divine. I ate an awful lot of it.

Then a very stupid but quite major problem arose – a small infection on my big toe was starting to get much worse and soon I was limping around with a massively swollen and painful toe, hardly able to walk. The plans to do some trekking had to be cancelled and I told my French friend to continue without me. Usually I was strong enough to fight off infections but this one really took hold so I was reduced to just hanging out in tea shops and little restaurants and chatting with the mixture of people who were passing through. I limped around the town a bit but it was not very interesting: some old wooden building covered with carved patterns and these tattered flags flying everywhere. Best were the Tibetan people who had escaped from Tibet. They touched me with their dignity and strange beauty. I loved the jewelry that they made and sold.

When wondering quite what to do with myself, someone suggested that I take the postal jeep up to the Chinese border as I could just sit in the vehicle and admire the scenery. Unfortunately Liz was off on a short two-day trek so she couldn't go with me but I was assured that other people would be going on the trip so I wouldn't be alone. I had to go to the post office at about 5am and when the old unroofed jeep finally looked like it was about to set off I realised that there were no other western passengers, just locals. There were a few Nepalese women and two Nepalese students who had been studying in Australia so spoke good English. They told me I had nothing to worry about. The jeep would reach the Chinese border to deliver mail by 11am and would be back in Kathmandu by 5pm at the latest. Simple! What could go wrong?

As everybody else seemed to be very cheerful and friendly, I decided to continue. As advised, I gave the driver half the payment, telling him that I would pay him the remainder when we returned. The journey up the mountains was certainly spectacular. Monsoon rains were not long over so there were waterfalls everywhere and the foliage was green and lush. The hillsides were sculptured with layers and layers of rice paddies following the contours of the slopes and, although the rice had already been harvested, the paddies were still full of water so they reflected a rainbow of colours: the blue and white of the cloud-studded sky, the green of the vegetation and the colours of the inevitable flags. It was glorious.

As we passed small, very poor villages, passengers got off and by the time we reached the rather ominous Chinese border, complete with uniformed guards, I was congratulating myself on a good decision and looking forward to the journey back.

Just before the border post there was a little village where we stopped, the driver got out and disappeared – for lunch, I presumed – and a local woman came out with curd and bread to sell and chai to drink Nobody spoke English but I managed to mime that I needed a toilet and one woman took me to a primitive hole-in-the-ground affair which wasn't the greatest but served its purpose.

When the jeep driver finally came back to his vehicle, with a trussed-up live chicken in his hand, I was the only passenger but we picked up two more men as we drove back down. And then things started to go wrong and I started to feel that I could be in trouble. After travelling for about an hour there was a lot of conversation amongst the passengers and something seemed to be decided because in the next small village the jeep stopped and everyone got out, the chicken too, and took off. I waited and waited and waited – for three hours! When the men finally came back at about 4pm they were very jovial and had obviously been drinking, even the driver. I had calculated that it would soon be dark and my scenic drive was just about over and I would only get to Kathmandu at about 8pm. Maybe.

My calculations were wrong because after another hour there was another stop and the men disappeared again. It was now dark and I was sitting there alone, freezing cold, on a mountainside at the mercy of whatever these guys had in mind. Worse was to follow as, after a further two hours, another six guys joined the original three and so now I was accompanied by nine drunks. Fortunately they ignored me and I just hoped that there would be no more stops.

It was now totally dark and the driver was driving with gay abandon down the narrow mountain road with sheer drops on the side. We then reached a level part and the vehicle stopped. What now? But the driver hadn't stopped the vehicle and it soon dawned on everybody that the jeep had run out of petrol. Much laughing and joking ensued, more discussions and apparently they decided that the best thing to do was to turn the jeep around and reverse down. It took me some time to figure all this out. I could only think that with the jeep angled in this position the remaining petrol would flow to the bottom of the tank and might be sufficient to get the jeep across more level ground when it wasn't free-wheeling downhill. They gestured to me to get out while they pushed and shoved and slowly manoeuvered the jeep into a reverse position. So now the jeep was reversing down this pitch-black narrow road with no lights, no gears and a drunken driver. I was terrified.

There were many stops and starts because when the petrol finally ran out the men simply had to push! Finally I could see the lights of a small village, a huge cheer arose and the jeep came to a standstill. Again they all disappeared leaving me sitting alone in the dark. I could do nothing else but accept and wait. Eventually the driver and another man showed up carrying a can full of petrol which they proceeded to pour into the tank. Laughing happily, the driver and friend then jumped into the jeep and we drove into the small village to pick up the rest of the passengers.

Or so I thought. Again I was wrong. Apparently everyone had been invited to a meal and more drinks. Except me. I still sat alone in the open jeep, frozen to the core and ravenously hungry. It seemed that the nightmare was to continue and I truly wondered if I would survive.

When we finally got back to Kathmandu, after a slightly less hair-raising ride because the road was wider and no longer winding round the side of the mountain, it was 4am – twenty-three hours since we had left that morning. When I got out of the jeep, stiff with cold and exhaustion, weak with fear and hunger, my toe excruciatingly painful, the driver actually had the cheek to ask me for the rest of the fare. I let him know in no uncertain terms, using every four-letter word I could think of, that I was very definitely NOT going to pay him and limped off down the deserted road to the hotel. As I walked I reflected that I was totally alone in this place and completely at the mercy of all those drunk guys but I think my fury protected me because they didn't follow.

I of course slept the whole of that day and finally woke in the evening to find Liz returned. With a friend close by I could tell the horror story with more equanimity and she was gratifyingly shocked and commiserative.

I was ready to leave Nepal the next day but Liz persuaded me to stay and accompany her on an easy hike to a kind of outlook camp on a hill not too far away from where you could see Mt Everest. You slept in a kind of shed and awoke before dawn to see the sun rising over the mountain. So we set out for this place in the early afternoon, thinking it would take about four hours to reach it. It took much longer, maybe because my toe was still painful and hampered my progress. We had to climb a small hill but before we were half way up it was really dark, so dark we could see nothing ahead of us and we soon knew that we were lost. By now it was very, very cold and I really started to panic, having visions of us dying of exposure on this cold hillside. Nobody knew where we had gone so there was nobody to even sound an alarm and sophisticated rescue services were non-existent at that time!

Fortunately, before we got too cold to move, a light suddenly appeared through some trees about half a mile up the hill and we started to shout for help. Along with answering calls, the light started to make a jagged descent towards us as we put on a final spurt of energy and climbed up on hands and knees to meet it. It was rough going as we weren't on any kind of path but when a very nice man finally reached us with the torch, the going got easier and by the time we finally reached the top we had warmed up nicely with the exertion. There was small barn which could sleep about twenty people and there was almost that number gathered there. Inside was a big log fire and some Nepalese people serving hot drinks which were very welcome. Needless to say we slept soundly even though the floor was hard.

It was worth all the effort to wake up the next morning to see the famous mountain right there in front of us, lit by the rays of the rising sun. We lingered a long while there, enjoying the clear views and chatting with some really nice people. The pleasant time continued as we all walked down another way though fields and small villages where the locals were going about their daily business and were full of smiles. My hitherto rather negative views of the country were somewhat modified but not enough to keep me there and I decided to leave the next day for Patna and Benares. I had had enough of the cold and my sights were now set on some Goan sun and sea.

There was a well-known bus that travelled through the mountain passes to India so I caught it, finding to my relief that there was another western couple travelling too. It was a pretty standard rugged journey with infinite stops for punctures and engine trouble but we arrived in Patna after a fourteen-hour trip and I had just time enough to catch a train to Benares where I knew I could stay with Kavi and Kavida.By an astounding miracle my money had arrived! I felt almost weak with relief as I now had only about fifty rupees left. I had to receive the money in cash because the Bank of India didn't issue travellers cheques because in those days they were only available at two American Express offices, one in Delhi and one in Bombay. I would have to carry this thick wad of money with me until I got to Delhi. Very dangerous.

My usual method of carrying money was in a cloth purse I had made which I attached to my knickers with a large safety pin. My passport and change was in another bag strung around my neck inside my shirt. So much cash made a thick wad which made me look a bit pregnant and it was fortunate that it was now quite cold and I could wrap a shawl around me, Indian style, to hide the bump.

I was determined to be on my way as soon as possible and, after repaying Kavi for the air ticket, I went off to the train station and was very lucky to get a ticket for a sleeping berth in a 'ladies compartment' to go to Delhi that night. In India a 'ladies compartment' was just that: a compartment for unaccompanied ladies to protect them from the ravishes of unknown prowling men! Peace and no hassles. I slept quite well and arrived in Delhi the next morning, happy to be going south to the sea.

Delhi to Goa – by train and boat

a leisurely sea journey, an abundance of fruit,
a primordial beach, an untouched Goan paradise

Chapter 10

Arriving in Delhi, my first action was to get a ticket on a train to Bombay (now Mumbai) as soon as possible. After a four-hour wait in the queue I managed to get a seat in a ladies compartment the following day. It was a thirty-six hour train journey so a berth enabling me to sleep would have been preferable, but I was lucky to get even a seat at such short notice. Indian ladies were often very kind so I hoped I might at least have a chance to have a few hours sleep on someone else's bunk at some point.

The second action was to go to the American Express office and buy traveller's cheques as I didn't want to be carrying so much cash around. Also the black market dealers preferred traveller's cheques and gave a slightly higher rate for them. In those days, wherever you went in India, you had people hassling you and saying 'Change money? Change money?' so it wasn't hard to find the right places. However, it was imperative to be extremely careful with these guys as their main purpose was to rip you off as much as they could so the whole exchange in some back room was a major battle of wits and you needed to stay totally alert and ready for any games they might play.

Then I went back to the hippie place I had stayed at before and made a reservation for some floor space. Rectangles the size of a bed had been painted on the floor and numbered, so you reserved a numbered space. You didn't dare to leave your

115

bags there – not only did the locals steal things, hippies did too – but it was possible to check your backpack in at the reception office (for 'office' read tiny room where the 'proprietor' lived, worked, ate and slept) so that you didn't have to lug your luggage around with you.

It was rather a relief to be back in the relative cleanliness and 'civilisation' of Delhi and I went straight to an English bookshop and bought a copy of Tolkien's 'Lord of the Rings' which was now all the rage amongst my hippie contemporaries. I hoped this would provide some entertainment on the long journey ahead of me. I also stocked up on Britannica Glucose Biscuits to keep hunger at bay. It was not a good idea to eat the food provided at various stations along the route as it was usually inedible due to its chilli content and also very unhygienic. With the filthy substandard toilets on the trains, one did not want to have to visit them frequently because of diarrhoea. Bananas were safe to eat if one peeled them carefully without touching the fruit, and Britannica Biscuits and banana 'sandwiches' were a mainstay of one's travelling diet.

I slept late the next morning as I still had the whole day to while away until I could catch the train in the evening. Finally it was time to leave and I boarded the train and found my ladies compartment, to the huge interest of everyone concerned. I think that due to these experiences, I have an idea what it must be like to be a celebrity and have all eyes on you wherever you go and whatever you do! A young western woman travelling alone in India was a real novelty. The ladies in my compartment were as usual very kind and welcoming and embarked on the inevitable interrogation process because they all spoke English to a certain degree. Only reasonably well-off Indians could afford this second class level of travel and these ladies were usually fairly well-educated. I answered all their questions as best I could but soon it was time to sleep.

It was a long journey and I was very grateful for the book. Ladies got out and in at various stations along the way so I was constantly having to explain myself – but it helped to relieve the boredom of the trip. I was lucky the next night to get a top berth for myself as someone had not arrived. This was fortunate because I was not sure what would happen once I arrived in Bombay so I needed all my wits about me. A good night's sleep would help. Via the hippie grapevine I had heard of a boat that one could take from Bombay to Goa and I planned to go that way if I could. It was supposedly quite a beautiful trip for a very low price if one slept on deck. But I didn't know where the boat left from or the schedule so I was a bit tense about the venture.

Although I didn't realise it at the time, it was fortunate that the train was punctual. Trains in India usually kept to a hypothetical schedule rather than a real one but this train was running on the main line connecting the two largest cities in India so its timing was reasonably reliable as many important people used it. Internal air flights were rare and only for the very rich.

I got ready to get off the train as quickly as possible to try to catch that boat so I was only dimly aware of the quite extraordinarily beautiful Victorian-style building that was this train station, called appropriately Victoria Terminus. I later found out that it had been built by the British to commemorate the Golden Jubilee of Queen Victoria in 1887. At that moment I wasn't interested in its merits; I needed a person in some kind of authority who could give me the information I required. I was relieved to see a Government Tourist Office just outside the building and even more relieved when the young woman behind the counter seemed to know about this boat. To my consternation it left at 9 o'clock – I had an hour to get there and I had no idea where to go. But the young woman rose to the occasion by writing out detailed instructions in Hindi, complete with a small map, which she told me to give to a taxi driver.

This I did and a cheery taxi driver waggled his head and took off for the harbour. He forced his way through all kinds of barriers and inspection points and finally stopped outside a small office. He of course expected a good tip and I obliged but told him to wait (my Hindi was good enough for this) until I knew I could get on the boat. To my surprise and relief, I could, and the deck space cost a whole nineteen rupees – under two pounds. Not bad for a three-day and two-night journey.

And so I boarded the nearby boat, staked my claim on the deck next to some ladies and their children and watched the departure proceedings as the boat moved away from the quay. I could just see the Gateway to India monument and the famous Taj Mahal Hotel next to it before we moved south. Then I took a very deep breath and relaxed. I was on my way.

It really was a very beautiful journey. The boat sailed leisurely down the coast within sight of land all the time. From time to time we passed picturesque fishing boats – like dhows, I suppose – with interestingly shaped sails. For the first time since I had been in India things moved in slow motion and it was extremely restful just sitting there in silence looking at the vast expanse of sea and two sunsets. It was wonderful to slow down and know I didn't have to go anywhere, do anything or see anybody for the next few days. A real holiday after the fantastic but very strenuous past few months.

As it turned out, I wasn't totally the lone westerner on the boat because on the second day a very good-looking American guy called Toby appeared on my third class deck. He looked too clean and spruce to be a regular hippie traveller and indeed, he had arrived in Bombay by air only a week previously. It was nice to chat and he invited me to up to the first class deck to eat some proper food. The only food available in my lowly quarters was some chilli-fuelled pakoras and cups of chai. However, I found, to my surprise, that Toby was a fruitarian and so ate only fruit and nuts. I wondered to myself how long he would survive in India as fruit, apart from bananas, was a no-no as it harboured all kinds of germs unkind to the guts.

I felt revived and refreshed when the boat finally docked in the Goan capital of Panaji around midday. It was like a different country! The buildings looked European and the people wore western-style clothes. There were not so many of them either, so I could actually walk rather than shove my way through teeming hordes. And they didn't hassle us at all, only glancing at us as we walked along the palm-tree-decorated quay. Very restful. I decided immediately that I was going to like this place -- very much!

John had said that he would go to a place called Calangute which was apparently one of the areas where western hippies congregated and Toby thought that might be a good place to start. Even the buses here were in reasonable condition in contrast to some of the wrecks I had travelled on before and it is difficult to express the contentment I felt at being back in a tropical setting close to the sea. I had been brought up in the tropics so this was my natural habitat.

I know what Goa is like now and, except for a few remote areas, it tragically bears almost no resemblance to the Goa that was then. At that time it was virtually untouched by western or Indian tourism. It was like a little encapsulated island with its own unique culture which was derived from the Portuguese influences in the sixteenth century but blended into something entirely its own. The road wound its way through thick plantations of palm trees and cashew nut trees with glimpses of endless rice paddies in-between. It was totally pure in its primitiveness. The bus finally turned seawards through a narrow dirt road bordered by palm trees, slowing every few yards for people, children, buffalos, pigs and millions of chickens to get out of the way. I was entranced.

We finally arrived at a deserted beach with a few houses dotted around and a chai shack. I had been told to get out of the bus and wait until a local came running to offer you a room for the night. This is exactly what happened and for two rupees each we got a clean room sparsely furnished with some pegs on the wall for clothes and two single beds made from wood and rope. Adequate simplicity. We then started food negotiations. Despite my Hindi – which, although not the local language, was used and understood – it was very difficult to make the family understand Toby's requirements of fruit only and we finally compromised by ordering one simple meal a day for two (which I would divide and eat for lunch and dinner) and lots of fruit. Fruit was easy! We had arrived at a paradise full of fruit and from all accounts it was fairly safe to eat. Maybe Toby would be all right as long as he stayed here.

The accommodation was only temporary because I didn't really want to live with him – I would prefer to be on my own and then hopefully connect with John – but for a day or two this would be fine.

The next morning, as excited as a child, I got up before sunrise and walked along the beach which was bustling with the fishermen hauling in their nets full of the early morning catch, and locals waiting to pile the still flipping fish into baskets to take them to market. It was such a timeless scene. As the sun rose more people arrived, along with the local vendors, and I bought my most favourite fruit, a papaya. I had been brought up on papayas but had not had one for many years. I also bought some bananas and nimbu, the little green lemons so common in India, and a loaf of home-made banana bread. Breakfast was served.

A few westerners were in evidence but none had heard of an American called John. They told me, however, about an abandoned building on the cliff just past Baga Beach, across a small river, which had been taken over by some hippies who wanted to form a commune there. Perhaps John was with them. I decided to investigate right after breakfast.

Toby slept a lot – perhaps because a fruitarian diet was rather lacking in essential nutrients so didn't provide much energy – and he fortunately wasn't interested in my expedition. I was free to wander off down the beach alone, rejoicing in the blue sky, the clean air and sea water and the happy lack of human beings. A Google satellite map now shows this area to be one endless urban sprawl, but all that I saw then was a glorious mixture of palm trees and banana trees which sheltered an occasional hut made of woven palm leaves. Pigs and piglets snuffled around and now and then a child ran out to wave.

When I finally reached the small river I could see a building up on the cliff and waited for the ferryman in a small canoe- shaped boat to reach my side of the river and ferry me across. I climbed up a cliff and walked into the building where

I was greeted by some people who invited me to join them in the creation of this commune. I had never heard of such a concept and felt it wasn't for me but I admired their idea and enjoyed their company. Nobody had heard of John but one woman said that there was a group of musicians living in a house on Vagator Beach which was further up the coast. I apparently had to first take a bus to a small town called Mapsa and then hitch a ride on a motorcycle 'taxi' to the beach.

This sounded very promising so I decided to embark on that journey the next day.

Back in Calangute, Toby had met up with some people who were planning to rent an old house and had invited us to join them. As it had six rooms we could each have a room to ourselves. This was the start of the real estate boom in Goa! Over the next few years, as Goa's fame spread, more and more people arrived and the locals took the opportunity to earn some money by renting out houses. But at that time there was almost nothing available and most people built small huts from woven palm tree leaves and grass mats – some quite picturesque.

I liked the idea of having my own room so said yes, although I told the people that I wanted to first go to Vagator Beach the next day to see if I could find a friend.

After my early morning visit to the beach and the ritual papaya breakfast, I set off to walk up to the main road to catch the bus to Mapsa. Half way up I saw a man walking towards me and was amazed to see it was John! He told me that he had had a feeling that I would be around somewhere and, as he had told me to go to Calangute, he thought he had better go there as well to see if he could find me. The timing couldn't have been more perfect.

He was indeed staying in the musicians' house in Vagator and invited me to come and join them. He said Vagator Beach was more wild and beautiful than Calangute. So we went back to my room and I packed my backpack once again. The very sweet family were sorry to see me go and I felt a bit bad about deserting them as I knew the money I paid them was quite important. But when I slipped fifty rupees into the lady's hand (a month's rent), bright smiles broke forth and I left with many heartfelt goodbyes.

On the main road, chatting excitedly all the time, we waited for the next bus for which, naturally, there was no set time. When it came, it came! That was it. Finally it did arrive and for the first time I heard the refrain which I can still hear today: 'Mapsa! Mapsa! Mapsaaaaa!' I loved Mapsa. It was a plain but busy little place and we spent some time exploring the small market where I had my first fruit juice. Goa was later to abound with fruit juice bars – if a man could get the money together to buy an electrical blender, he was in business – but this was the first time I had seen and tasted them. You could concoct any mixture you fancied as fruit was in abundance everywhere.

We also visited the cashew market. At that time the sale and export of cashew nuts was big business and one of Goa's chief sources of income before the influx of tourists. The cashew plant was brought to Goa from South America by the Portuguese in the 1500's and the English word 'cashew' comes from the Portuguese name for the plant: caju. The outer shell of the nut or seed is acidic and dangerous to human skin so gloves have to be worn when extracting the kernel. But the roasted, salted nuts were delicious and we naturally bought a lot. Due to aggressive tourism and so much building, the cashew nut forests have now almost entirely disappeared.

Then there were little shops selling brightly coloured saris, lunghis and other cloth, and cooking utensils and ornaments made from coconut shells.

As there was no road to Vagator, neither buses nor cars could get there. The only transport was provided by young guys on motorbikes which could navigate the rough track. It was a bumpy, rather hazardous ride into what seemed to me a tropical jungle. It was certainly more wild than Calangute and I was surprised that a house even existed here. I suppose it was a kind of plantation farmhouse – presumably the land belonged to somebody.

There was a small community of six westerners living in the house, most of them musicians. It was a very romantic, idyllic existence but when we went down to Vagator beach the next morning I knew I had found my place. There was a cove with white untouched sand which ended in a great pile of rocks all spiked and jagged like something out of 'Lord of the Rings'. There was something really primordial about it, like an undiscovered, untouched desert island. We were the modern day Robinson Crusoes.

When John showed me a cave at the back of the beach I decided immediately that I didn't want to sleep in the house, I wanted to sleep here. Only occasionally in my life have I experienced such a sense of pristine purity in a place. I spent about ten days living in that cave. It was a magical time being so closely in touch with nature: sitting on the beach witnessing the rising and the setting sun, the rising and the setting moon and everything that happened in-between. I loved also to sit on the rocks as the tides rose and fell, sometimes covering most of the rocks, sometimes just leaving shallow pools. Up on the cliff there were some ruins of an old fort from where one could see across the mouth of the Chapora lagoon to an untouched land, devoid of any human beings, on the other side. You really felt sometimes that you were the only person on the planet. It was an extraordinary feeling.

One lazy day followed the other. We bought fruit and vegetables and the inevitable banana bread from the locals or went on shopping trips to Mapsa. A faint cry of 'Mapsa! Mapsa! Mapsaaa!' would cause someone to jump up, grab a bag and run to catch the motorbike taxi on its return journey to the 'big city'.

There was no such thing as running water. We shared communal wells with the locals for cooking water. As we were naked in the sea for at least a few hours every day, bathing wasn't an issue but every few days we went south to the next beach which had a waterfall of fresh water which fell into a small pool and provided a good washing place to soak the salt from the sea out of one's hair and off one's skin.

The toilets were a source of great hilarity. Unlike the rest of sewage-strewn India, where it seemed that any open space was a potential toilet, the Goans were fastidious about sanitation and had created a perfectly ecological sewage system. Small grass huts, erected at convenient intervals, were built on stilts a few feet above the ground. One ascended two or three steps and sat on a wooden bench with a hole. There was usually no door so one could happily sit watching the whole tropical scene in front of one. This was fine. The unnerving thing about it all, however, was that the sewage disposal was the job of the local pigs who, as soon as they saw someone heading for the hut, ran as fast as they could to position themselves in the space below the hole, ready to devour whatever fell from above. Looking through the hole before one sat down and seeing two or three pigs, snouts raised expectantly, took some getting used to! I was already a vegetarian but even if I wasn't, I most definitely would not have eaten pork in Goa.

With the influx of western tourists this brilliant system eventually broke down as the poor pigs sadly became ill and died from the not so pure, often amoeba-filled, deposits left by foreigners. After a few weeks it was time to return to a more mundane world and face India again. John wanted to go on a journey or pilgrimage to visit the home of an Indian mystic called Meher Baba, in a place called Meherbad, near Ahmednagar in Maharastra State. He said he would be back in about two weeks. As I didn't want to stay in Vagator alone because I wasn't into playing music, I decided to return to Calangute and hopefully find a room in the house where Toby was staying. So we regretfully turned our backs on paradise, found Toby's house where there was fortunately still a room for me, and John set off on his pilgrimage. I didn't know that I would never see him again.

I still enjoyed Calangute. It was very different from the isolated Vagator but it had its own unique flavour with the fishing boat scenes in the early morning and the locals going about their simple daily tasks with such calm contentment.

Then, one morning, sitting silently and watching these timeless scenes, I was approached by three men and was suddenly shocked into a totally incongruous western energy and thrown back into world that was now so far away and almost forgotten. It seemed that they were an Italian film crew making a film about hippies in India and they wanted me to be in the opening scenes – something about a hippie wedding – that they were filming the next morning. I of course said 'no'. What a strange reality. But later in the day they came to the house and begged us all to be part of the film. Toby and the others thought it was quite a joke and decided they were up for it as it was a novel twist to our daily existence. With them all agreeing, it was difficult for me to hold out and finally I gave in and nodded an 'okay'.

I had no idea that with that nod and that 'okay' my life would, within a week, totally change direction and my remarkable wanderings on these less travelled roads would come to a sudden end.

That, though, is a further story.

Appendix

For more photographs and reviews about this book,
and for information about the two follow-on books
in Veena Schlegel's trilogy
(*Glimpses of my Master* and *A Mountain in China*)
please see:

www.3books.co.uk